From Pieces

to

Peace:

Damaged Goods

Written by Robin Major-Oliphant

From Pieces to Peace: Damaged Goods

www.one2mpower.com

ISBN:9781986069205

Disclaimer: I would like to thank my real-life reasons, seasons, lifetimes… family and friends portrayed in this book, for loving me and supporting me one way or another throughout this journey. I realize that their memories of the events described in this book may be different than my own however, the pertinent details are factual and are described to the best of my ability without dramatics. Names, characteristics, and locations have been altered to protect the privacy of everyone but the author. The book was not published as intent to hurt anyone.

From Pieces to Peace: Damaged Goods

<u>Content</u>

This book is dedicated to every reason, season and lifetime that has come into my life, may you continue to go forth and impact lives in a positive way. To anyone feeling broken, tainted, damaged, unworthy or anything less than what you were created to be. While it may not seem like it just yet, if you stick with me long enough you will see just how this entire journey is for and dedicated to each and every last one of you...but for now please know you are enough because God created you to be. To anyone suffering in silence with depression, or silently suffering from domestic violence or abuse of any kind, please know that you are not alone. My prayer for you is that soon you will become your One (One2Mpower); speak up and get help in the meantime, I pray that I can somehow be your One through the words of these pages. I love you all and thank you for supporting me as I use my testimonies to inspire and empower you.

Peace, Love and Light,
Robin Major-Oliphant

Roadmap to Damaged

I really wish I could say life hasn't always been rough. However, the first memory that comes to mind about my childhood is the pain of being molested by my uncle on that cold, bathroom floor. For most of my young adult years, I allowed the hurt of that memory and the sexual abuse of my brother to subconsciously affect the choices that I subsequently made in the future. While ambition and an inherent will to succeed have always been my strong points, bitterness, resentment and playing the blame game were the evils that kept me in a place of repeating the cycle of making damaging choice after damaging choice for the majority of my adult life.

There were plenty of fun times, laughs, loving moments and celebrations growing up. We had family reunions, birthday parties, holiday gatherings and other family functions. After my grandmother passed when I was fourteen, those good times and memories came to an end. Without her, it was hard to see the good in anything. I had fewer and fewer good times to keep my mind away from the bad ones that I had gone through in the years before she passed. My mind became increasingly tainted with old memories and heartache. I dwelled more on thoughts like those of being beaten, sexually abused by my brother while we watched porn, my mother turning a blind eye to my abuse and her own and picking at the emotional scars of being left behind by my absentee father. But there was one memory that ate away at me for several years. Mostly because it was never spoken about. It was the memory of going for a ride with my mother's friend to grab ice cream and we ultimately ended up in another county being dropped off at child welfare. At this time, we were placed into foster care because my mother was no longer ready to be a parent. She preferred the fast life of partying, drugs and unhealthy relationships after she and my father divorced. Part of that life included the company she kept. In retrospect, the friends she allowed in her life and mine influenced as well. Although it was not my norm, my mother was aware that I was an occasional drinker and I dabbled with smoking marijuana. I had been exposed to that type of environment growing up around my mother and her friends during my younger years so that is what I had equated to "fun". Whenever it was time to have fun and the opportunity to drink and smoke presented itself, I went for it. I'm intelligent, but failed to decline the chance to get high with my 7th grade best friend and her mother. Since I witnessed my mom and her friends having fun smoking, I didn't want to be the party pooper. I also had the same mindset Homecoming night during my senior year in high school. I drank, smoked, and pretended to be someone I wasn't. These are just two of the many times I didn't protect who I genuinely was and conformed to the person my friends wanted me to be at the time. My mother taught me how to party and pretend. Those lessons I held on to for years to come.

As a child, I never knew which mom I was going to get. For instance, it was my birthday kickback during senior year and she was doting on me. It was one of the happiest days of my life but yet a night that I will never forget. We were getting along, she loved on me and acted proud of me. It felt so good because everyone was there to celebrate me. In contrast, there were times like Homecoming, which was during the same week when it was as if I had no mother. It was time for the dance so I got dolled up. She hadn't bothered to come home and see me off for my senior year Homecoming dance. It was my last dance and I hadn't heard from my mother. I was cute! I wanted her to be there. I wanted her to celebrate with me. I was hurt and perplexed. I started to think of reasons why she wouldn't want to be there. Furthermore, I quickly dismissed any of those thoughts and cracked my signature, bright, fake smile for pictures. I wish she would have been consistently hot or cold, but she was lukewarm. Having a lukewarm parent left a nauseous feeling throughout my life.

My mother had mastered the art of wearing a mask. However, the problem was she had come accustomed to wearing so many that I'm sure this woman had no idea who she was most days! The influence the men in her life had over her would make her unpredictable. She suffered physical abuse at the hands of boyfriends, brainwashed and wearing a different mask as the relationships changed. With every new relationship my mother entered, she took on a new persona. One of my mother's fiancés, who she later married and divorced, had an extraordinary influence on her life. We got into a fist fight the summer of my junior year because he paddled me. I was cleaning the kitchen and as he was passing through to go out of the back door, he began to meddle with me. He always picked on me and did things that made me feel uneasy like randomly licking my face. His touch made me cringe. I assumed he was going to lick my face since he was so close so I pushed him away and said something under my breath causing him to get agitated. Then, he began to fuss and I ignored him. He felt disrespected and demanded I give him the response he wanted, or he would paddle me but I still refused.

I stood there quiet and slid down the kitchen cabinet and waited for him to get back with his paddle. Meanwhile, I watched as my mother stood by not saying or doing anything. When he returned, he shouted his command to me once more and I ignored him. He counted to three as if I would change my mind, but I had checked out. I braced myself as he grabbed me by my arm tightly. He turned me around and hit me across my butt once but I didn't flinch. The second time, I don't know what came over me but I decided to fight this registered boxer with my fist! I hit him with a one two punch in the face before he tackled me. My mother never interceded until I threatened to call the police. She called them instead, as I was being slammed and dragged. She never said a word, never offered any help and never protected me. I thought my dad would come and rescue me once I told him, but that didn't happen.

When officers arrived, I begged to be charged and taken away. They attempted to convince me how bad jail would be, but I didn't care. Once I calmed down, the officers pulled me aside and talked about the consequences of having a record at my age. I agreed to stay home even though it meant living under the roof of a woman who was loving one day and failed to protect me the next day. I reminded myself it was only for a season. I ran up to my room and cried. I called my uncle Tony to tell him what happened so he came over to confront my stepfather. At the end of it, my mother called me a liar. I was placed on punishment but it felt more like a jail sentence. When it was over we went back to "acting" like a normal family. We never spoke of this day again.

Somewhere in her life, my mother had been silenced. She was now teaching me to be quiet along with the art of pretending just like her. I didn't know it then, but I learned later that I was subconsciously putting on masks too. I don't know when it started, but I always recognized when other people wore them. I saw straight through my mother, my father and my oldest sibling because I knew them. However, I don't know when I began to evolve into someone I wasn't. But I do know the more comfortable I got with being someone else, the more comfortable I became with layering the masks. Somewhere on this path, I'd become a chameleon. I was going through life changing who I was to fit others' ideas to gain acceptance, to gain love and to feel less damaged.

I've endured enough abuse to last a lifetime. I now wonder if there was an unseen roadmap laid out for me. For generations, family members have followed the same course. When I was in my adolescent years, my mother sat me down to discuss the abuse she endured. Full of emotion, she told me her mother's boyfriend had molested her. Then he threatened her and my grandmother's life if she was to tell anyone. My emotions were full of ambivalence. I felt angry at her for seeking sympathy from me about her past abuse when she refused to hear me when I told her of my uncle's abuse towards me years prior. Nonetheless, I still empathized with her because I could see she still bore unhealed wounds from her own abuse.

My mother did not provide all of the gruesome details, but I later learned my grandmother was also a victim of domestic abuse for some time. My mother's point in telling me about her abuse was to "teach me" to speak up if someone ever touched me, regardless of how they threatened me or what tactics they used to keep me silent. Her words fell on deaf ears. I had already been silenced by the one person who was meant to protect me on earth. But she too was a victim of this vicious cycle of abuse that seemed to be a generational curse that was rooting itself in our family for countless years. It was affecting countless women, men, boys and girls while silently passing down from generation to generation within our family. This underground railroad of abuse and silence was damaging us all.

I'm not sure what my mother's issue was in her abusive relationships. I always wondered why she stayed, or if she even knew that her children knew she was being abused. I never tried to understand the abuse as I child; I only wanted it to end and for my mother to stop hurting. I needed her to stop running the streets long enough to pay attention to the hurt I was being subjected to under the roof of her house.

Silenced

"What goes on in my house, stays in my house!"

Chapter 1

Silenced

As a child, I was taught to stay in a child's place. "What goes on in my house, stays in my house!" This still resonates within me so much so that I now bitterly realize I too have echoed it to my own children. Have I silenced them about something as significant as abuse? I will never forget during my first grade year, a social worker came to our school to educate children on child molestation. Children who felt they may have been abused were encouraged to stay behind and speak with the social worker. Initially, I was hesitant and feared being in trouble or rejected. My uncle never threatened me but I knew what he did was wrong. I also knew telling would hurt my family. Years had passed but I was still hurting and I wanted to heal. With a nauseous belly and my mother's voice in my head, I kept hearing her say, "What goes on in my house, stays in my house!" I hesitantly reached out to the social worker and told her I "thought" I was a victim of sexual abuse. I don't remember the full conversation, but I do recall her reassuring me I had done the right thing and was not in trouble. I felt free after telling her but my freedom was short lived. When I arrived home, my mother asked me, "What did you tell those people at the school?" I timidly responded, "Uncle used to touch me in the bathroom at our old house when you and dad were not home." "You don't know what you are talking about! That never happened" she replied. My mother made it clear to me, and the school, that I had made the whole story up. Because of this, that was the last I ever spoke of it. I was so young and the urge to rebel wasn't in me. Since I was just placed back in my mother's home after a few months in foster care, I was mostly afraid of her more than anything. I had been silenced. I didn't know then she was damaged and was only doing what she had been taught to do...be silent.

This should've been a pivotal moment for the healing I desired. I'd finally spoken of one very heavy, dark, and scary experience. It was a heavy load for a first grader. Instead of progressing toward healing, another piece of my spirit died. I needed my mommy and she wasn't there. How could I, a child, heal from something I could barely describe without the love and support of my own mother? How could I escape feelings of being violated? How would I overcome the spirit of fear and being timid? How could I walk boldly with my head held high and chest out when I was tainted? Sadly to say, I wouldn't have the answers to these questions for many years.

After being rejected by my mother, I couldn't process any of my emotions. I just knew I didn't feel protected by her. I began to cling to one of my brothers for protection. I was confident he would continue to protect me like he did in foster care when our foster-father pushed me into the pool as a joke, knowing I couldn't swim. My brother jumped in to get me out and we told the social worker what had taken place. He knew I needed protection then and I needed him to protect me again. However, he was unaware that I even needed him to protect me at this time. He was the very, protective "big brother". The one who stood up for me and showed me affection. I don't remember my exact age but I was around nine or ten years old when he began to change. He went from being my protector to a predator. My mom was in an abusive relationship at the time and I would hear her fighting with her boyfriend. This made me afraid, and I'd often wet the bed. In an effort to escape the madness, I sometimes snuck in my brother's room and slept. This happened frequently and over time, my brother began to abuse me. I now found myself suppressing the need to speak up for myself once again. I still carried the memory of what happened when I advocated for myself before. The silencing my mother gave me had made me voiceless. It was as if she had taken away my larynx. Nothing could come from me, not even screams.

I would lie silently as he touched me. Even as it progressed from touching to intercourse, I never fought, I never squealed, I just laid there. He used manipulative tactics by telling me that if I didn't do what he wanted, he would tell our mother on me, as if I was the one taking advantage of him sexually! That put so much fear in my heart. When my mother shut me up about my uncle, she seriously shut me up. It was the true definition of paralysis. I was too paralyzed to even take the risk of my mother knowing and rejecting me again. I feared she would believe I was the one abusing him!

Not only did he abuse me, he persuaded others into doing the same. I remember distinctly when two of my male cousins came over to spend the night. My brother wanted them to "try it". The youngest of the two was about nine or ten, and he didn't under any circumstances want to "touch" me but my brother bullied him into raping me. I remember us all being in my brother's room and he put Vaseline lotion on my genitalia, and told my younger cousin to "go ahead". All I can remember is being absent from myself as my cousin entered me from behind and thrust a few times and it was over. Thankfully, my older cousin did not go forward with it. I think they may have told their mother since they never came to visit us again.

For some odd reason, I never forced my brother to get off of me, nor did I verbally say no. I just took it silently, often dealing with the mental and emotional battle until it happened again. I continued to be silent until I grew weary. Sometimes, I found myself getting enough courage to stop my brother from raping me. I somehow stopped being afraid to sleep in my own room. Sleeping in his room out of fear gave him easy access to me. It took me a while to figure out, "Robin, just don't go in his room." If he called for me to come in there, I found the nerve to tell him no. I don't know if his room was his "safe place" or not, but not going in there decreased the sexual abuse but made the bullying, manipulation and physical abuse worse. By now, he was much bigger and taller than I was. His size intimidated me along with the fact that he was a boy. He would bully me throughout the day, take my dolls from me and break them, punch me in my chest and dare me to hit him back. He called me names and allowed his friends to taunt me too. He used to protect me from bullies, but now he was one. I used to tell my mother, "You need to get him some help, he is going to be a woman beater!" All I received was chastisement for speaking ill words against his life, but I was really just crying out for help. Nevertheless, my cries fell on deaf ears. Although it seemed impossible, I was silenced even more. The more damage being done to me, the more silent I became.

It often felt like I was living in a war zone when it came to him. For years I didn't fight back, until one day, I had enough! Enough rape! Enough bullying! Enough beatings! Enough being silent! ENOUGH! As a single mom, my mother worked all the time so my brothers and I were home alone what seemed like 24/7. Day in and day out, I had to deal with this menacing preteen who got a rise out of making me miserable. He wanted me to do something like iron his clothes, but I just wasn't having it that day. He always gave warning "Robin, if you don't do_____, I'm punching you dead in your chest!" This day, I just stood there waiting for it! I was ready for him to knock me dead, or for the

Spirit of the Lord to rise up in me so that I could kill him! I stood there unmoved.

He got angry and did the usual. He punched me so hard in my chest, it knocked the wind out of me. I don't know what came over me or where I got the strength from, but I broke the leg off of the ironing board and beat him with it until I couldn't beat anymore! I grabbed the phone and ran to the basement and hid inside the clothes dryer to call my grandmother. My will to live had kicked in and I did not want to suffer at the hands of this beast anymore. I had clearly hurt him and his pride.

"Gramma!"

"Yes? What's wrong?"

"Please tell Ashley to come and get me now before my brother kills me!"

My grandmother said, "What happened?!"

I replied, "He is gonna kill me hurry up!"

When Ashley arrived, my brother was gone and she took me to my safe-haven. It was one of my most favorite places in the world-Grandma Marie's house. On the way there, Ashley asked what happened with my brother and me. She got a real kick out of the story as I told her play by play, how I had beaten him with the leg of the ironing board. It was funny to see him squirm on the floor! While I was scared for my life during the altercation, sharing the story with my cousin brought a smile to my face. That was the last time I had problems with my brother. It wasn't always sunshine and skittles but at least he wasn't sexually violating me or putting his hands on me. The verbal bullying and name calling I could deal with.

Evicted

"...you have 2 weeks to get out of my house!"

Chapter 2

Evicted

Senior year and all its festivities had arrived! The week of Homecoming and my birthday consisted of constant celebrations for my friends and me. To start the festivities off my mother had thrown me a birthday celebration at the beginning of the week. I called it a "kickback". It was an unusually beautiful day out, unseasonably warm, the birds were chirping, people were riding down the street in their convertibles with the tops down and music blaring. It felt like summertime was back already just for this special day, my 18th birthday. I had invited my friends from everywhere to this impromptu kickback, I'm talking homeboys from the Northside of town, my boyfriend Antoine and his friends from the Southside, all of my friends from both Collingwood and Telegraph High had come to hang out. I was lucky to have gone to school in the city, and later transferred to a differed school on the West side of town so I had an eclectic mix of friends from just about every corner of the city who I had invited to come and enjoy the shenanigans with me! We had plenty of good food, great music, entertainment and lots of laughs.

My Uncle Tony also came by, and he brought some Cuevo 1800 for himself but I managed to sneak a few celebratory shots for myself behind the scenes. My friends and I eagerly talked about homecoming night which was that upcoming Saturday, our hopes and plans for going away to college and just growing up and getting out of the city! A few of my friends were already graduated and on the college grind so I just could not wait for my moment to really get out of the city, and figure out what the world had to offer me. A few of us had already had the opportunity to get a taste of what college life felt like by way of the Onward Forward college prep program we attended during the school year once per week, and for six weeks out of the summer on the local college campus, so we were excited to experience the long term effects of what college had to offer and how it would impact our future.

My birthday kickback was a night that I will never forget, and as simple as it may sound it was one of the happiest days of my life. My mother and I were getting along, she seem proud of me thus far and everyone was there to celebrate, encourage and uplift me, it was a really good feeling. My Aunt Margaret; who is notorious for making sure that she takes pics or records EVERY family function, did not disappoint and made sure she brought her camcorder and recorded every memorable moment, from us laughing and cracking on each other, to us dancing and carrying on. My Aunt Margaret overheard me and my friend Sheila talking about our plans for homecoming night which included staying out all night long, and hosting a hotel party (I know, doesn't sound like a good idea but as a teenager it sounded like the best idea at the time). When I noticed that my Aunt was eavesdropping on our conversation, I invited her and her camcorder into the conversation and reconfirmed announcing belligerently; and obviously a little intoxicated but serious just the same,

"Attention, Attention everybody! Ma, you too… I have an announcement. I will not be coming home after homecoming Saturday night, I repeat! I will not be coming home Saturday night after the dance, so don't wait up! We are having a hotel party afterward!"

Once I ended my announcement people who didn't know what my plans were wanted details, they wanted to come to the party with us!

We had plans to make Homecoming night the highlight of the week and the hotel party afterwards would be the grand finale. I already let my mother know my after party plans, and there were no objections made by her. The Homecoming dance was everything I had hoped it would be and more! Even though my boyfriend wasn't my date, I had the time of my life! After the dance was over, we mingled a bit in the parking lot for a while and headed out. We all hopped in the car, picked up a bottle of liquor, some lemon juice and headed to the hotel. We drank, sang, laughed, smoked a little and recapped the high points of the dance while heading to the hotel. By the time we got there, I was hammered and all I wanted to do was sleep. Bummed that I had passed out, upon awakening the next morning, my next thought was that I needed to get some food and some Tylenol because my head was hurting very bad. I asked my friend, Brooklyn, to take me home. As soon as I walked in the house, my mother exclaimed "Where have you been?!" I was instantly irritated and caught off guard by her tone because she already knew where I was and because I had the worst headache known to man! I nonchalantly said, "Ma, you knew where I was. I was at the hotel. We had a hotel party. "She quickly responded, "I didn't know nothing about no hotel! But since you want to be grown and disrespectful, get dressed because we are going to church!"

We went back and forth for a minute, mostly me pleading with her and trying to remind her of how I told her about the party and how she said ok, and how Aunt Margaret even had it on video tape. She got even more agitated. It was like the more I reminded her, the more she tried to shut me out. She finally abruptly ended the conversation, "Since you want to be grown and stay out all night, you have 2 weeks to get out of my house!"

I would spend the next two weeks on punishment. I spent the duration of that time reading, writing poems, listening to music, and sitting on the porch. On the last day of my punishment my favorite cousin had come over. I was in my room getting ready to go to the movies with Antoine when Ashley came upstairs to talk to me. I told her that my two weeks were almost up, and I had nowhere to go. She didn't believe my mother would put me out. Apparently, no one in the family who heard about it believed she would do it even though she painted a picture of lies about me. She lied to them about not knowing where I was, who I was with and told them I was being disrespectful! I couldn't understand it. My mom was accusing me of being with Antoine, while other people were questioning the entire situation. Antoine knew I wasn't with him, and of course I knew that I was with my friends. Friends who were my witnesses at my birthday get-together the day we all talked about where I would be Homecoming night. This entire ordeal made me feel ostracized by my mother, again. She'd consistently told family, "Since she grown, she got to get out!" I spoke with Ashley a little while longer and left for the movies.

After we left the movies, Antoine and I went to a bar to talk. Although I wasn't in love with him, one day at a hotel bar I found myself telling him about what happened in my house over the course of two weeks. I was breaking the rule of "what happens in my house, stays in my house."

I hadn't told Antoine what had been going on with my mother and I, but I got the feeling that he sensed something was bothering me. I opened up and began to tell him that my mother was threatening to kick me out of the house, and I wasn't sure when because she could be so unpredictable. I told him that she had given me a two weeks' notice, and I would literally have to pack my things and leave. Antoine was somewhat understanding, nodding and sipping his drink. He tried to reassure me that I wouldn't be put out on the streets. We talked a little longer, and he asked questions that I couldn't answer. I couldn't tell him if my mother would really put me out, nor could I tell him why she didn't believe me when I told her she was aware of my plans that night and knew where I would be. I couldn't tell him anything, but that my time was almost up. I began to feel like he wasn't on my side, and started to clam up. We left the bar and rode in awkward silence.

When we pulled into the driveway, the view was heartbreaking. Awaiting my arrival were neatly stacked clear totes and boxes full of all of my personal belongings. I am convinced both Antoine and I heard my heart break into a million pieces as we both looked on at the porch. It looked like delivered packages at Christmas time. I cried and cried. I was officially a homeless, high school senior with a $6/hr. job and nowhere to go. I was frozen, dazed and in total shock. I could not believe I had been put out my mom's house. Furthermore, I still had one more day!

Antoine immediately began to pack my belongings in his compact car in the pouring rain, but I couldn't bear to watch. I asked him to stop and to get me out of there. I had nowhere to go and had no idea what I was going to do, but I had enough family so someone would take me in. Maybe even my dad would let me move in with him in Michigan. We headed to Antoine's sister's house. Upon arrival, I began to call family members based on how much I thought they loved me. I started with my dad.

"Dad, my mom kicked me out!" After sharing the same story, play by play, I popped the question, the same one I had asked a time or two before.

"Dad, can I move up there with you?" My dad's response was probably the most heartbreaking of them all, "No baby, I can't do that. I can't have you coming up here disturbing my household because of what you and your mom have going on." That response took me at least 10 years to get over. I just didn't get it. How can he tell his homeless child that he cannot take me in? How could he not at least take a night to sleep on it? I had so many questions! How could he go on and build a new life with new kids and leave me living in misery with a mother who seemed to show no love? How could he leave me with a mother who always chose men over me? Was he trying to damage me even more? My resentment for him ignited beyond measure! I began blaming him for mistakes that I would make in the future, only calling him when I needed him and hoping that one day he would see where he had failed me as a father.

I went on to call two of my aunts and a cousin who I believed really loved me, just to be turned down because no one wanted to get in the middle of what my mother and I had going on. It was hard to accept this coming from close family, so calling friends or any other family members who I wasn't that close with wasn't an option. Besides, I was not excited to lay my head in anyone's home. While it had been several years since I had been sexually abused, it was a recurrent fear that it may happen to me as an adult. I would later have a teacher offer to let me come live with him, his wife and kids, and I considered it but my spirit wouldn't let me. I felt uneasy about it. Years later, he went to prison for sexual misconduct with a minor; boy, did I dodge a bullet! I embarrassingly let Antoine know what my fate was and he reassured me that he would take care of me, but we would have to stay with his sister until Monday. Two days later, he'd gotten us an apartment, had it fully furnished, and picked up the rest of my things from the back porch of my mother's house.

Chapter 3

Accepted

Damaged goods often take what we can get. Even if it is a tainted, half-done relationship that isn't quite right. We weigh the pros and cons and even when the bad times outweigh the good, we are still grateful for the few good times we have. Antoine was mild-mannered and a seemingly good guy who was a sweet, silly introvert. He graduated a few years before I did. I loved that even though he was older than me, he never pressured me for sex and just allowed me to be me. Our relationship was about fun and enjoying each other. He made me feel loved and while I wasn't at the point of loving him back just yet, I knew he loved me, and that felt good. When it came to dating, I was very selective and didn't just date anyone. I liked the ones who accepted me and made me feel comfortable. Antoine genuinely accepted me.

Antoine and I had been dating for five months and were not sexually involved. So I think as a gentlemanly gesture, he slept on the couch when we first moved in together to make me feel comfortable. This definitely put me at ease because while I was not a virgin, I was not sexually active either. The last thing I wanted to do was complicate my life by becoming emotionally tied to Antoine by getting wrapped up in the bed with him. I just wasn't in love with him, and I definitely wasn't about to have casual sex either. Besides, I still wasn't sure how I felt about sex at this point in my life. He loved me and I liked him a lot. However, I knew he wasn't my future. I knew I wanted to go away to college and I wanted much more than Toledo. Getting wrapped up in a relationship with him would only complicate things.

Our one bedroom apartment was cute and perfect for a young couple. Our furnishings were all black--black sectional, black tables, black décor, and black bedding. *That was all Antoine's doing. But we were young and figuring things out and at the time it worked for us.* Our new residence was about five miles away from my high school and right on the bus line. Antoine was able to drive me to and from work most of the time so I didn't miss a beat! I had to take two buses in order to get to school in the morning but I was willing to do whatever it takes to get away from Toledo and that meant finishing high school. So if I had to walk to the bus stop in the cold and take a couple of buses that was what I was willing to do.

My senior year was supposed to be one of the happiest and most memorable times of my life. However, considering all that had taken place, it was beginning to become a bit of a blur to me. The days seemed to fly by as I went about my routine. Go to school, go to work, back home, go to bed...repeat. I didn't hang out with my friends much outside of school and Antoine and I really didn't do much anymore since we were now shacking up. It seemed like our dating life had pretty much come to a halt. The awesome senior year I had hoped for now became bleak.

Nearly a month had gone by, and although my mother and I didn't have the best relationship in the world, I missed her, my home and my family. I think this was my first onset of depression. I was simply going through the motions pretending to be ok when in reality, I was broken inside. I had no way to express myself and I felt like no one cared. Antoine was being good to me. I liked and appreciated him; however, I was not at all content with living with him. I learned a lot about Antoine that I did not know before and those things were not things that made me particularly proud to be his girlfriend.

One thing I learned in particular was that he loved to smoke weed every single day! At the time, I had no problem with him smoking weed in his spare time, but I didn't realize that everything and everyone else came after his habit. Nonetheless, I had dismissed my feelings and concerns. Who was I to judge him? He had taken me in, was taking care of me, paying all of the bills, cooking, cleaning and everything so I really had no room to complain. I thought I didn't deserve better because of all that I had been through. I think this was my first experience at settling because he had accepted me. I thought that because I had been sexually abused and tainted, I didn't deserve much more than what I received. Since he accepted me, I felt it was what I deserved. I was damaged. I needed to be grateful.

Thanksgiving was my first holiday away from family, and I spent it with Antoine and his family. We were playing cards, drinking daiquiris and having adult conversations that often left me feeling awkward and uncomfortable. I was totally out of my element, but I convinced myself to embrace it and just go with the flow. Thus, I just flowed right into drunkenness.

When we got home, Antoine helped me into the shower and that helped to sober me up quite a bit but not enough to suppress the sexual desires that were coming out of nowhere. I was sobered up but my inhibitions had been released and obviously so had his since he was waiting for me to return from the shower. As aroused as I "thought" I was when it was time to get down to business, I just laid there with tears streaming down my face. "What the heck are you doing?! I thought to myself, "Did he even put on a condom?" Afraid to ask, I just laid there, lifeless, not making a sound while allowing him to penetrate me as I try to figure out ways to avoid an encounter the next go round.

That night, Antoine slept in the bed with me for the first time and held me. I was conflicted because we were grown and doing what grown-ups do right?! Nope, wrong! This was all wrong, all of it! I screamed on the inside! I felt dirty as if I were committing the ultimate sin; yet, I still laid there saying nothing as he slept peacefully like the happiest man on earth. I was in "like" with him, and surely appreciated him for being a provider and putting a roof over my head. Nevertheless, I just wasn't sure that I was in love with him. How was I going to get myself out of this??? We began sleeping in the bed together nightly. Although he tried rubbing up against me here and there, I typically feigned sleep and he rarely pressed the issue. Before I knew it, Christmas had come and gone.

The night after Christmas, my friend Sheila, called me excitedly asking me to go to the store to pick up a pregnancy test with her. She and her boyfriend, Michael, had been dating for years by now. As crazy as their relationship was, they seemed madly in love with one another and she was dying to be pregnant for some reason. We were really close friends but she and I had two totally different mindsets as it related to college, sex and life in general. I had post-graduation plans for my life and sex really wasn't my thing in high school. On the contrary, she was looking forward to working and starting a family with Michael after high school.

I agreed to go to the store with Sheila since I had nothing else to do. Besides, I had no interest in seeing my family and Antoine was with his family. We arrived at the store and lingered around for a bit before sliding into the bathroom with two stolen pregnancy tests. My period was nine days late, and although I wasn't worried, I decided to take the test in moral support. After we finished taking the tests, we both came out of the stalls super excited. I was super excited and relieved my test was negative, while Sheila was excited to finally be getting her baby. We slipped the toilet paper wrapped pregnancy tests in our coats and scurried out of the store.

The next morning, as I was getting ready to rush out of the door to ride with Sheila to the pregnancy clinic, I reached into my coat pocket and felt the pregnancy test. Before going into the bathroom to triple wrap it to prevent it from being seen inside the trash, I unwrapped it one last time to take a second look just for final assurance. I was amazed, perplexed and downright pissed off at what I saw before me. The test now read POSITIVE!!! This had to be some sort of sick joke Sheila was pulling on me, but it wasn't. Who knew December 27th 1999 would be the first day of the rest of my new life?!

Here I was a high school senior, and I had just turned 18 years old, with no idea how to be a young lady, much less a woman. I had no clue how raise a child. To make matters worse, out of nowhere, the man who had been the knight-in-shining armor had turned into a blame-shifting weasel. His only solution to dealing with the pregnancy was to terminate it. I was not emotionally equipped to even consider having an abortion. My choice to carry this life drove a wedge between us. Antoine was unsupportive and ultimately blamed me and "my" pregnancy for his inability to finish the college classes that he barely attended. Meanwhile, I was seven months pregnant when high school graduation came around and Antoine didn't even bother to show up to the graduation ceremony.

During my third trimester, my pregnancy took a turn for the worse. I was in and out of the hospital and felt it was best that I go back to live at my mother's house in case I went into labor while Antoine was at work. In addition, if my mother or her husband weren't home, there was other family nearby.

It was awkward being there because I had not spoken to her much since October. It had been over nine months since I'd been evicted from her home. Since being evicted, there was a cloud of bitterness looming over our relationship. I was still hurt, but we made some level unspoken amends. The birth of my daughter kept the mood light because my mom was there to help me with her.

I presume the stress of becoming a parent caused Antoine to care less about the responsibilities of taking care of the bills at the apartment. Unbeknownst to me, while I was at my parents recovering from the birth of our daughter, he lost the apartment in an eviction and all of my personal items in the process; this included sentimental pictures, my high school diploma and other things that meant a lot to me at the time. Once this happened, I knew our relationship would never be the same. I chose to fight during that very terrifying time in our lives and he chose to fly by avoiding any conversation, financial responsibility or emotional support that was required of him.

After faking to mend my estranged relationship with my mom and step-father, I knew I needed them. I had nowhere else to go after I recovered. My mother helped me get my own low-income-based apartment in town. I tried briefly moving forward with Antoine in an effort to be good co-parents. I thought I was giving our daughter what I didn't have, a stable, two parent home. Although the relationship was loveless, I thought it was the best option for the sake of our daughter that we try to be together. I made sure Antoine paid the bills and pulled his own weight, but I knew it wouldn't last. He even made it his business to put himself on child support just in case things did not work out between us. I eagerly obliged because I knew the relationship would fail. He had very ambiguous, get-rich-quick schemes, but nothing ever came of them. He lacked ambition to see anything beyond being stuck in our city.

On the other hand, I was still looking forward to getting as far away from Ohio as I possibly could! Despite the fact that my mother had repeatedly told me my life was over since I had a child, she admonished me to forget about plans of going to college or the Reserves. She made it a point to drill into my skull that my life now revolved around my child, and I no longer had a right to my own dreams and ambitions. Part of me had given up hope, even though she had beaten me mentally, there was something embedded deep inside that never gave up. One year after giving birth to my daughter, I went to Community College because regardless of what my family told me, my life was not over. I was determined to defy the odds at all costs...period! I went off to college and out the door Antoine went! I had no time to keep faking it with him. We were engaged to be married for the sake of our daughter, but I didn't love him and never did. This was going nowhere fast. I had to move forward and pursue a better life for my daughter and I. No longer would I simply accept what I could get. I wanted more.

Damaged Dreams

"The entire trajectory of our lives can be changed by just one choice we make!"

Chapter 4

Damaged Dreams

Community College was all about taking care of business. Get in, get it done and move forward with pursuing your career. Student life wasn't impressive for me at all. There were no dorms, no sororities to get involved in and no clubs to join. From the logical perspective, this was perfect for me. I had a child and always held at least two jobs in the beginning of my college career. I didn't have much time to have a true college experience anyway. Nevertheless, my heart still yearned for the college life I had hoped and dreamed for. My close friends were experiencing it and that deepened my yearning for it too. Once I found a good balance and became more comfortable with my responsibilities as a parent, I found ways to party with my friends who went to nearby universities. I would spend weekends on campus with my friend, Kita and others, partying and hanging out while my Aunt Kim cared for my daughter. Those weekends spent on those campuses were bittersweet, mostly because I wanted to attend a major university. I wanted to pursue my four-year degree, pledge a sorority, and plan my future after graduation. I dreamed of my relocation to Los Angeles, California, where I planned to live in a one bedroom condo and gallivant around the city in my sports car only having to care for myself.

My reality was that I was a townie, living in low-income housing, taking care of a child, living paycheck-to-paycheck and not the life that I wanted to live. It was safe to say that while I partied, smiled and had some great times, my heart was still hardened. I was bitter and partially stuck in the 80's with the little molested girl who never had a chance. I was simultaneously stuck there and stagnant in the past few years due to the rejection and hurt from my mother and father. It was as if I was in some kind of emotional and mental limbo time warp. I wanted to move on, but remained in two past periods, while attempting to focus on my present and have hope for my future. The torment I was experiencing could barely be described with words. I blamed my parents for me getting pregnant. It was their fault I had to attend a community college instead of a university like I originally planned. It was their fault that my dreams had become damaged and my options were limited or taken away. With all this resentment and bitterness, I pressed on and tried to adapt to this reality that had been giving to me. I had to press or perish, and I couldn't afford to lose anymore of myself to life.

Getting through college wasn't easy. In fact, it would take me five years to complete a two-year program. The length of time had nothing to do with my intellectual abilities. I had always done well in school, regardless of the pain I suffered after that bell rang. College was hard because I had no idea what I was doing! No one sat down with me and told me what to expect, how to choose a program, how the student loans would rack up, or how to balance college, parenting and still be a young woman having fun. By the time I chose a program, I had already been in school for over a year. I worked multiple jobs, went to school full-time and partied at night. Luckily, I had a work-study job at the library and was able to study there. I deemed partying as a necessity because it was my escape from responsibility. As my history dictated, partying was my view of a good time. I was a party girl who loved music and dancing. Wednesday through Saturday of most weeks, I found myself at the club taking advantage of their featured drink specials. I was trying to force this party lifestyle to give me something it could never provide, while my Aunt Kim raised my baby.

I often had feelings of confusion, resentment and bitterness. This caused me to question why my mother didn't teach me everything I was now learning the hard way. I was learning how to be a woman, a mother and how to just "do life" alone with no solid foundation. It felt as if I was trying to build a life on quicksand. With my mother, there were no lessons of wisdom given. I didn't know what a healthy relationship looked like and I didn't know how to deal with this life I had. How could I still make my dreams come true if she didn't teach me that I could? How could I be a mom and a baby at the same time? I began to become internally upset with my mother for even the smallest things such as: not teaching me how to shave my legs, cook or even Dating

101. Someone had to take the blame for me being oblivious of "how to" do what seemed like all of "real life".

My dream of being a single, business professional who lived and loved life in California had been altered. My dream now included me wanting to be the best mother I could be. That dream was damaged too because of my lack of foundational teaching. Damage had already gotten a head start on me. Dreams I didn't know I had were already damaged by the time the dream entered my life. I knew nothing of being a parent. I knew nothing about nurture or affection. I didn't have any of that instilled in me from my parents. My mother was present in body only, and my father wasn't there in body or mind. Out of all the lessons I had been taught about, how to be a parent was the very one that would damage my newly discovered dream of being the best parent I could be. I wanted to be nurturing, loving, and a teacher to my child. I wanted to be able to be free enough to allow her to experience a life that I didn't have, and never learn the dark lessons that I had learned.

The pain of the past molestation and sexual abuse didn't only overwhelm me emotionally, it also reeled its damaging head in the way I raised my daughter. I spent years being an overprotective, overbearing, sometimes too hard, helicopter mother. I parented from fear, not from love. I feared the world preying on my child. When it came to her hugging, touching or being around men, I was extremely overprotective.

In all honesty, I didn't even want her to attend sleepovers because I was paranoid and afraid! My own damaging ghosts of the past were still damaging me. That old pathway that was laid out for me seemed to be the path my ghosts and those that birthed them were compelling me to stay on.

I spent years of my dating and child-rearing life not learning how to be a mother, but rather trying to be the polar opposite of what my mother was. In some cases this worked. However, it took me awhile to learn how to effectively be a nurturing, loving mother. I longed for a close relationship with my own mother. I wanted to miss her hugs and kisses as a child, but I couldn't miss something I didn't have. My mother wasn't affectionate at all. It was almost impossible for her to teach me something that she didn't have within her at the time of raising me. I didn't outwardly realize that I had not learned or received these things while I was growing up until it was my turn to raise someone.

Whenever I tried to figure out how to lessen the effects of my damage by self-reflecting, I often wondered what if I had ignored my mother's demands to not bring up the molestation by my uncle. What if I had kept telling people until someone believed me? What if I didn't trick myself into feeling like it was too late? What if I had told her about my brother? What could I have done to change the course of my life before now? The entire trajectory of our lives can be changed by just one choice we make! I had several opportunities in my past to be heard but chose to stay silent, bitter and resentful towards my mother, father, uncle and brother. Feelings of fear, hurt, embarrassment, and shame took a deeper root as time passed on. The root of bitterness and those deeply rooted feelings bore fruit of unhealthy choices and excuses for the bad choices I made.

I spent the next ten years of my life bitter! Bitter about old damaged dreams and the new damaged ones. The bitterness I felt pumped through my veins and into my very soul, and I internalized it all. Why didn't I ever get to go away to college? Why didn't I go to the military? Why didn't my father try to intervene when I reached out? Why couldn't I be the parent I wanted to be without fear? Why were my dreams being damaged? Why didn't someone protect me when I was going through an abusive relationship and fighting for my life? How did I even get to the point of fighting for my life?

Chapter 5

Entangled

One night, my friend Regina and I had gone to *Club 2000* to have a drink. It was a Tuesday night, and we didn't plan on partying hard. We just wanted to chill at the bar and mingle. At this time, I was in a really good headspace. School was going great, my partying had slowed down a bit, and I was just focused on completing my degree program so that I could move away from Toledo. While we were at the bar, two gentlemen walked up and asked Regina if anyone was sitting there and she politely told them, "No". Both men sat on the right side of her as we continued to converse. After a few moments, the guy sitting directly next to Regina offered to buy us a drink and we obliged. Small talk ensued; however, I was uninterested. I had been seeing someone but nothing exclusive and I wasn't pressed to meet anyone new. When the drinks arrived, the second guy came and sat next to me. He was 6ft 2in tall, attractive, medium build, brown skin, dark features, and a clean cut goatee with curly hair. "What's up, I'm Rodney. What's your name?" he inquired. I played friendly and since he wasn't from the area, I engaged more than I normally would have. Rodney told me that he was from Atlanta and had two children who lived there as well. Mentally, I'm excited because I wasn't into dating. But when I did, I made sure the kid's mothers were at bay. We talked a while longer and exchanged numbers before saying our goodbyes.

Rodney and I talked frequently throughout the following week. He invited me to a rap concert that upcoming Friday night, and I excitedly accepted the invitation. The concert was jam packed and I learned that night Rodney was a social butterfly. He knew everyone! He knew more people in the city than I. This had me thinking, "I thought he wasn't from here?"

Everything made sense when my old, high school classmate walked up to me and Rodney and said, "Hi Robin! How you been?" I was excited to see Hannah since it had been a long time. Grinning from ear to ear with my arm candy next to me, I excitedly responded, "I'm doing good girl...I can't complain." Hannah asked "Are you here with Rodney?" I began to think something must be wrong with him. I told Hannah I was there with Rodney as I began ushering her away from him to get the skinny on him. She burst out into laughter as I attempted to gain privacy to get more info on Rodney. Her quizzical facial expression when she asked if we were there together, was telling that she knew more than I obviously did. Our exchange was only about seven seconds long but it felt like an eternity before speaking. "That's my brother, girl!" she laughed even harder when she realized I was clueless to that fact.

It all came back to me! This was 'Rodney Rodney'! Fine Rodney from back in high school, all of the young girls had a crush on him. He was Hannah's older brother! Feelings of unworthiness started to flood my mind again as it always did. Should I tell him about my past? Should I keep it to myself? Surely something was wrong with him to choose me? Couldn't he tell I was damaged?

When we left the concert and went our separate ways, I went home, showered and all I could think about was Rodney. I had only met this guy earlier this week, but I lusted for him and began envisioning myself in a relationship with him. Was I delusional? It didn't matter because moments later my phone rang and it was him inquiring about what I was doing, as if we hadn't left the same place an hour ago. He asked if he could come over, and I gladly said, "Yes." I pondered as I prepared for his arrival. Could I get him to fall for me before he could figure out that I had been damaged? Before he found out that I had a past that often tormented me emotionally? Without a doubt and delay, I knew I could!

Rodney and I rapidly got wrapped and tangled up into each other. I was in love with this man and he totally adored me. He always complimented me on how beautiful I was and our sex life was intense. I saw Rodney's adoration for me as an act of love and respect. He was my protector and my friend. Whenever I would go out to the club where he was working, he tended to keep me close and I saw nothing wrong with that at the time. While mingling with my friends, I often checked in with him. It all seemed typical to me.

My mother, on the other hand, didn't like Rodney. I vividly remember when I took him to meet her at the house. She was divorced and living alone by this time so I introduced them and left the room to load the washer. Rodney looked uncomfortable when I returned and motioned that is was time to go. We got in the car and he blatantly said, "She don't like me." I quickly responded "How do you know?!" He said he just knew. I called my mother later that evening when Rodney wasn't around because I wanted to dispel the feeling Rodney expressed. "Ma, Rodney thinks you don't like him." I chuckled half-heartedly but she bluntly stated "I don't!"

I responded, "Why? You don't even know him?!" She swiftly snapped, "I don't have to know him. I just don't like him. There is something about him." After an awkward pause of disbelief and attempting to shift the conversation, I was unable to shake the discomfort so I ended the call with her.

That was the beginning of the resumed distance that occurred between my family and me. I spoke to my mother when I needed to, which was sporadic, and I rarely went around family. If she was not going to accept the one person who I thought finally made me happy, then surely I wasn't going to subject him to being around them. Little did I know, this would become a part of the vicious cycle. A cycle my mother had already come to know so well but failed to lend a warning to me about. There was no smoke signal or anything. But I'm not sure that I would have listened anyway. I was thinking I could get Rodney to fall in love with me and entangle him in my web. Nonetheless, he had me entangled in his. I was busy trying to hide my imperfections and he had been hiding his too.

As we experienced our highs and lows, I learned more about Rodney. It was becoming more evident he wasn't the perfect guy I allowed myself to believe he was. He obviously wasn't from Atlanta if he was the Rodney I had been head over heels for as a young girl. He grew up right in Toledo, Ohio. Since we had met, he hadn't even gone to Atlanta once. I was puzzled how he was seeing his two children if he never went there. He began to blame their mother but said the children would be moving to Ohio soon to be with him.

He always said and did all of the right things to right his wrongs. When I suspected him of doing wrong, he went out of his way to smother me with love, affection and time, until I felt as if I couldn't breathe. He would appear so sincere and genuine leaving me no choice but to believe him. He even told me he needed me and I believed him. He made me feel beautiful, loved and accepted. Rodney always complimented my smile, my heart, told me how proud he was of me for being a "go getter" despite my past. It was a cycle of building me up then breaking me down. I didn't recognize it because I was so close and deeply entangled within his grasp. My vision was too distorted to see the toxicity of the relationship. I didn't want to abandon him, but I realized he needed to save himself and that I couldn't be his savior. Heck, I still hadn't mastered the art of saving myself! There were times that I was certain Rodney had stolen from, lied to and cheated on me but I had no proof so his manipulation and lies won every time.

I had become so engulfed in my relationship with Rodney that focusing on school had become less of a priority for me. My focus wasn't as intense and I earned a D in one of my classes. That was a failing grade for a 10-credit hour course that was only offered in the fall semester! I was scheduled to graduate in the spring! I was in total and complete shock! I was bewildered and reality hit me; it hit me hard! I didn't know how to cope and had no one to lean on. Subsequently, I went into a complete depression. Being with Rodney didn't make it any better. I went from smoking black and mild cigars to smoking cigarettes and was placed on depression medication by my doctor "to help me cope."

I didn't initially identify with being depressed. I just knew I was deeply saddened all the time. My heart was heavy and I cried uncontrollably. It was hard for me to care for myself let alone my daughter. After about a month, I began having chest pains and an accelerated heart rate. I even felt like I would stop breathing in my sleep so I decided to finally go see my doctor. He diagnosed me with anxiety and depression, then placed me on a couple of medications in the beginning. I took the medications for months and lived like a zombie. The feelings of depression and other symptoms had indeed subsided but where was Robin? I didn't feel like myself. In addition to all of that, Rodney and I were discussing marriage and starting a family! I didn't think that my chances of getting pregnant with all the medications in my system would be good. I made the decision to stop taking my medications, without talking with my doctor. Emotionally, I was feeling better. Besides, I wanted Robin back. Additionally, I wanted my body back because my sex drive had taken a downturn from the medication.

After my system was clear, Rodney and I had begun trying for our baby! This was exciting because I was actually trying to have a baby, instead of being surprised by a pregnancy. My mother was not thrilled, but it didn't matter because our attempt was unsuccessful. Rodney never seemed to understand why I didn't get pregnant right away. He often accused me of sneaking birth control pills, which made no sense. He even accused me of not wanting to marry him, which always left me feeling guilty even when I did nothing wrong.

Rock Bottom

"I NEEDED TO LIVE; it didn't matter

what I WANTED!!!"

Chapter 6

Rock Bottom

The night of what would have been my graduation was a rough for me. Ironically, ALL of my friends were graduating from their universities! I went from high to very low. I was happy for all of them, at least I wanted to be. Nonetheless, I couldn't be there to support them. I stayed in bed all day, without much to eat or drink. Even though I physically couldn't show up and support them, I managed to give everyone a congratulatory call. I was falling back into my depressive state and the thought of getting out of bed was too much.

I didn't go to one graduation party, nor one ceremony. I saved myself the heartache and embarrassment from them seeing the inevitable tears of envy that would seep from my eyes. I couldn't bare them seeing me like that, so I stayed home and cried my eyes out. Although, I had been accepted into my Surgical Technology program for the next fall, it didn't matter because in my mind I had failed yet again. I was so mesmerized by my relationship with Rodney that I failed that class. Another failure and another deep and seeping wound.

To add to the emotional anguish of the events of the day, Rodney had come over to visit. While trying to hide my emotions about graduation, he and I had an argument. I was already an emotional wreck, and his mantrum was the straw that broke this barely standing camel's back. The argument stemmed from my mood and not wanting to go out. It was a petty argument but like any other time, he was not willing to let it go because I wouldn't do what he wanted me to do. He threatened to walk away from me but I was already in a depressive state and not in the mood to be emotionally manipulated. I dismissed Rodney's mantrum, but I couldn't shake the fact that my life was not what it was supposed to be. Here I was 23 years old, with a child, living in government housing, and a community college flunky. I felt a lack of purpose, while everyone around me seemed to be going on with their lives happily ever after. Why couldn't I have at least a fair shot from the beginning? Why did I have to begin behind the 8-Ball? Why did I have to fight from the beginning of my existence? Why did I have to be damaged goods?!

One night, I grabbed the bottle of painkillers on the nightstand next to my bed and searched my thoughts for the will to fight, but I couldn't find it. I felt hopeless and confused. My emotions were all over the place and I thought for certain I didn't want to live anymore. I knew I was absolutely tired of failing, tired of being a disappointment, tired of not getting it right, and not knowing what right was. I was just tired of life altogether. I was exhausted from aiming and missing the mark. I had nothing left. I took the bottle of twenty pills and laid on the floor crying waiting for anything to happen. I'm not sure what I expected, but I laid there because I had hit rock bottom. I lay there waiting to be consumed by whatever dwelt at rock bottom. I was ready to die.

Moments later, something did happen. I heard my five-year-old daughter moving around in her bed. She slept in a twin bed that was made of a stainless steel-like material so I assume the screws were a bit loose since it squeaked when she climbed in and out of bed. I was jolted back to reality by the sound of that squeaky bed. I went in a fog, as the medication was beginning to take effect. I jumped up as quickly as I could from the floor to run into the bathroom and stuck my finger down my throat to vomit. I NEEDED TO LIVE; it didn't matter what I WANTED!!!

I continued to gag myself and vomit as much as I could as the white, bitter medication mixed with water began to come up. As I rushed back to my bedroom to grab the phone to call my cousin, Tatiana, I dialed swiftly. With tears streaming down my face, slurred speech, and still in shock, I frantically stated, "TT, I need you! Please, come get me now." Tatiana responded, "What's wrong, what happened?!" I could hear the empathy and concern in her voice, but I knew we didn't have much time to waste. I didn't have time to beat around the bush. "I just tried to kill myself! I took a bottle of pills," I exclaimed. That was all I needed to say.

I felt drunk, worried and terrified. As I await for the arrival of TT, I gazed into my daughter's room to see that she was still sound asleep. This freaked me out even more! I know I had heard her moving around. Had I lost my entire mind? What was wrong with me? I was much smarter than this! I was a warrior! I was never one to give up. What made me do such a thing?!

Tatiana and her mom, my Aunt Charlotte, rushed over and picked me up within moments. I don't remember much about the ride other than my Aunt Charlotte praying. I didn't feel judged or condemned; I just felt love. My aunt was a tender-hearted woman of God who truly lived her life like I believe He would want us to live. She didn't have a mean-spirited bone in her body and she was good to everyone. Aunt Charlotte was always there whenever the family needed her. I still truly believe because of how the events happened that night from the exchange on the phone with TT, to the prayers of her mother's righteous heart that is what saved me. I didn't pray for myself, not because I didn't want to, but because I was so filled with worry and painkillers that I just sat in the seat and listened. Hoped that some way, somehow my aunt's prayers would manifest and my body and mind would be restored.

Unbeknownst to me, when I was signing the "consent for treatment" upon hospital admission, I technically signed myself into the psychiatric ward of the hospital. Still a bit sedated from the lingering drugs in my system, I was not aware that I was being transported to the psych ward until I was instructed to remove my belt and shoelaces upon arrival to the unit. It was at that moment reality set in once again and I lost control. I began to kick, scream and attempt to get up from the wheelchair as the nurses, TT, and my aunt tried to calm me down. I began screaming, "LET ME GO!!!! I'M NOT CRAZY!!!!" The more they tried to calm me, the more I attempted to break free. With tears streaming down my already tear-stained face, "I WANT TO GO HOME!!! I'M NOT CRAZY!"

Aunt Charlotte's normally calm voice wasn't so calm at this point as she shouted, "Calm down! If you keep acting crazy, they will believe you!" Although I heard her, I couldn't process it. They'd made a mistake! I wasn't crazy! I was highly intelligent and had common sense. I was a mother! My child needed me! "I'M NOT CRAZY!!!" I continued to shout, but my scream fell on deaf ears. The nurse threatened to sedate me. There was something about her threatening to put me down like a dog that totally silenced me! I mean I completely shut up, almost like when my mother silenced me back when I was a child.

What was to be a few days turned into a couple of weeks in the psychiatric unit. My daughter was with Antoine while I was in the hospital. I hated he knew where I was and what I was going through. After all, I had left him because I wanted better for myself and here I was in the psych ward of the hospital while he took care of our child.

I didn't eat much at all; I just smoked more. Even though I told myself I wanted to stop smoking, my nerves had become worse and it was my way of coping with my anxiety. My thoughts had begun to consume me. What will people think of me? Not only had I managed to get kicked out of my mother's home before finishing high school, I graduated pregnant and had a baby right after my high school graduation. I flunked out of community college due to carelessness and was now in the "looney bin". That was just the outward, obvious stuff people knew about me. Surely I had become a statistic. Another damaged girl with a sob story that no one cared to hear about.

Kita, TT, and my parents came to see me a few times but no one else did, and I can't say that I blamed them. I didn't want to see anyone while I was in that place despite the fact that I was lonely and afraid. My family was sure to ban Rodney from visiting me because they assumed that there was something I wasn't telling them. When I did get a chance to communicate with him, he claimed he didn't visit me because he wasn't on the list. I believe we both just knew he wouldn't have come anyway. None of my family liked him at all. I guess they sensed the toxicity of our relationship. My family saw what I couldn't see. They saw the manipulation, lies, possessiveness, and the wedge he drove between me and them. I didn't realize the toxicity of our relationship because I was too close to it and too deeply immersed in my feelings for him while being intertwined in his web. Obviously, since my mother had her own experience of being a domestic violence survivor, she saw what I never saw coming. She never spoke up to save me. Maybe she thought simply saying "I don't like him" was fair warning enough, but it wasn't. It was just enough embers to keep my fire burning for him long enough to create a situation that would prove to be life altering.

Clear Proof, Damaged

Sight

"In all my winning, I was weak, damaged and settling."

Chapter 7

Clear Proof, Damaged Sight

Upon my release from the hospital, I spent time soul searching, and was in a quiet and subdued space. I was embarrassed about what I had done and I wasn't sure who I was, what I wanted or what I was supposed to do next. I was lost. Like clockwork, Rodney came back around and was the only person who seemed to be there for me. At this point, he had practically moved in with me and even started coming to my job for lunch. This experience seemed to have brought us closer, and resumed our unorthodox quest toward family planning.

Rodney and I spent the summer sexing like rabbits, aggressively trying to get pregnant but we were still unsuccessful. I had become discouraged, and the reality of being damaged began to set in once again. After I gave birth to my daughter with Antoine, my doctor advised me not to have any more children due to medical concerns. I had been diagnosed with pre-cervical cancer on more than one occasion, and I had undergone several outpatient procedures, each one removing more and more of my cervix. I learned that this would result in another high-risk pregnancy, which would put the child and I in jeopardy. Knowing my medical dilemma, compounded by Rodney desperately wanting more children, made me feel low. The more we tried and failed, the lower I felt. I quit trying. I put it out of my mind and began to focus on going back to school since I was accepted back into the Surgical Technology Degree Program. When the semester began, I was more focused than ever before. However, the more I focused on school, the less Rodney came around. Little did I know, Rodney had found someone else.

The first time I found out that he was cheating, I had stopped by, Club 2000, the club where he hosted parties regularly. I had stopped hanging out so much since I was really focused on finishing out the last ten months of my degree. I had stopped going out as often, so he definitely wasn't expecting me. I was scanning the club looking for him, but he was nowhere to be found. I knew there was only one place he could be, outside on the patio smoking a cigar. I stepped outside and several people were standing around engaged in conversations. I looked to my right to see him lounging in a chair with a young lady sitting on his lap. She was a 5' 5" chocolate girl, wearing a curly wig and a light, pink tight-fitted dress. Her back was to me, but he somehow saw me as I gazed at him. I turned away and walked back into the club and out the door.

Moments later, he called asking me to come back. I didn't go back; I couldn't because I was hurt and embarrassed. My thoughts raced, "How long has he been embarrassing me like this?" "How long has he been having a relationship with some other chick up at the club?" Then, feelings of insecurity rose up within me. I wondered what made her special. Were they having sex? Could she give him the children I couldn't? I was done until he came over and fed me the lies, which I ate up quickly. He told me she was a waitress taking his order, and if I would've came back, I would have found that out. Before long, we were in bed again. I partially believed him, but deep down inside I knew everything he told me was a lie.

After the night at the club, I came face to face with this young lady again. I had just left Rodney at his cousin's house and I saw her drive by me! I quickly turned around while frantically dialing his number, but he wouldn't answer. When I pulled to his house, the girl and her mother were standing outside as I approached. Cherice was her name and I got a better look at her. My heart sunk even more. What was I missing?! She had a slim waist, wide hips, a small chest, and a bad case of acne. She wasn't as beautiful as I had imagined her to be. I was 5'9", had a slim waist with a small frame all the way around, and was quite beautiful myself so I felt I must have been missing something. I obsessed over him leaving me for her and grew angrier every moment. Rodney decided to ignore both of our calls and refused to come out of the house.

Cherice, her mom, and I had an awkward conversation. I had found out that Cherice and Rodney had been dating off and on for nearly as long as he and I had been exclusive. The mother vouched for the claims and the conversation ended with her saying she was tired of Rodney's mess. We both hopped in our cars and parted ways. Fifteen minutes later, Rodney called me to explain how Cherice was crazy and lying on him. I listened to the lies…the I'm not cheating, the she's crazy, knowing all along he did cheat but still I stayed.

I didn't try to compete with Cherice. After all, I didn't need to and besides she said she was done and I undoubtedly knew I was the better choice. This wasn't about Rodney; it was about winning! Furthermore, in my mind, I had already won! I looked better on the outside, regardless of how damaged my insides were. I drove a better car, wasn't living home with my mother, had a job, and would have my degree in a few months. There was no comparison, and I needed that point to be proven. I stayed with him, and he made my presence known at all the clubs he worked. He'd shouted my name out over the mic and had drinks comp'd for me and my girls. Everyone knew Robin was with Rodney. I officially won!

In all my winning, I was weak, damaged and settling. Rodney was a fine man, but in reality, that's all he was because he didn't provide for me the things that mattered. It wasn't about the sex either since I wasn't into it like that. Nonetheless, I was emotionally attached to him because he accepted me just like Antoine did. Rodney made me feel loved and needed so I believed the lies and stayed with him. I had the proof that I didn't have before, but I was too damaged to completely believe what I saw. I felt somehow bound to him.

Life after the Cherice situation began to settle down. Things were starting to feel like they could be normal. Rodney got a job at a collection agency to help out because the money from the club was inconsistent. He also mentioned his son and daughter were coming to live with us, but I didn't really take him seriously. Rodney and I had been dating for over a year and I had yet to meet his children. This made it difficult to wrap my head around the idea of them moving in with us. Besides, I wasn't ready to add additional children to our lives. I still had plans on leaving Toledo and there was no reason to complicate my life with additional children who didn't belong to me. I knew if I loved Rodney, I should also love his children. However, it's also possible for me to love them and not want them to move in with me.

As a young adult, kids just weren't my thing. As a matter of fact, children weren't in my plan ever. I often wondered if my lack of affection for children had to do with the lack of affection that I received as a child. The only impressionable affection I received growing up was unwarranted sexual affection from my brother and whoever else he tried to force to give it a go. No "I love you's", hugs or kisses from my mom but lots of fussing and scolding. I guess it was in love, but it didn't feel that way at the time.

I was forced to babysit while my mother and her friends went out so I would later repeat the same cycle for a while. After having my daughter at age 18, resetting my sails, meeting Rodney and hearing his dreams of a big family, I wanted to have that matched burning desire he had to have the perfect, big, happy family; but I didn't.

Life was going great! Rodney and I weren't having any problems and he seemed to be faithful. On Christmas Day, I was sick as a dog. I didn't know if I had too much to drink the night before or if I had the flu, but I wasn't feeling well. Rodney went ahead to be with his family, and I stayed in bed after I sent my daughter off to her dad's house. Kita called me and I remembered I had promised to make mac and cheese for her family dinner. Therefore, I peeled myself out of bed and prepared my mother's signature mac and cheese dish. That was one thing my mom had done a good job at and that was teaching me how to cook over the phone because I didn't have the advantage of leaning side by side in the kitchen with her growing up. While Kita and I chatted, I let her know how awful I felt. She nonchalantly said, "You probably pregnant!" Un-phased or alarmed, I replied, "Girl I wish! I don't think I can get pregnant."

It took a moment, but after the conversation, I thought it wouldn't hurt to take a test. It wouldn't be the first time and if it was negative, Rodney wouldn't have to know I took it. I wanted to avoid the conversation of failing him once again even though I had pretty much given up. I went to the closest store, which was two minutes away from my house, and picked up a pregnancy test. Once the test was in my hand, I was excited and mad at myself at the same time for being excited. I know that sounds contradictory, but I guess I really didn't know what I wanted. At first, I wanted a baby. Then, I didn't because I thought I couldn't have one and now I felt the desire to have one again. I felt like a maniac.

I took the test and instantly it was positive! I was ecstatic! Kita was the first person I called, and when she came to pick up the mac and cheese, I left with her to celebrate Christmas with my best friend and her family. When I told Rodney, he was elated as well. He told everyone and it was an exciting and fun time. This was different than my first pregnancy because I didn't go into hiding due to shame. I wasn't an eighteen-year-old, high school senior anymore. I was an adult this time and I wanted this. I was with the man I loved, the man I was going to spend the rest of my life with, and the man who was going to marry me.

The Master Plan

"Smile, don't look so mean."

Chapter 8

The Master Plan

Valentine's Day was like no other. While I didn't have many plans, Rodney seemed to be uber excited about the day, despite the fact he had to work. I would often take him lunch when I didn't have class or work. Normally, we would go to a nearby restaurant or walk and talk when the weather permitted. Sometimes we would just sit in the car enjoying each other's company until his break was over. This day it was cold, and there was still snow on the ground. So I took him some food, and we sat in the car to eat. Although it was Valentine's Day, neither of us fussed over the schematics. We knew we would enjoy each other later on, over a romantic dinner before Rodney's comedy show event he had been promoting. The comedy show would be held at a club downtown called *The Master Plan*, it was upscale much nicer than their regular venue *Club 2000*.

After we finished eating, Rodney turned and looked at me and began telling me how much he loved me, before belting out a line from a song I had started writing for him a while back. "I love you, I love you, I love you, I love you, I love you...I love you, I dooooooo," he sang. I blushed as he pulls a ring box out of his jacket pocket; I knew what was coming! So many thoughts were going through my mind. It wasn't like in the fairytales, nor a moment full of awe, wonder, and tears. NOPE! I sat there hoping he didn't purchase the least appealing of the three rings we had looked at a couple weeks prior. Imagine my disdain when he opened the box and it was that very ring. While happy to finally be engaged to someone I actually wanted to marry, I was not pleased with the token of his love.

Since I wear my emotions on my face, Rodney noticed it right away. "What's wrong?! You don't like it. Do you?" Rodney stated sorely. I perked up with a soft smile, leaned in for a kiss across the seat, and told him, "I love it." I realized I was being ridiculous. After all, the ring could eventually be replaced but his love could not. His intentions were good, and he was attempting to make an honest woman out of the woman who was carrying his child. After his break was over, he went back to work and I continued my day as well. I was elated to be his forever.

I waited and waited for Rodney to come home so that we could go to dinner, but he never came. He didn't pick up the phone, which was odd and his phone went directly to voicemail when I called. As soon as I began to worry, Rodney came through the front door rushing to shower so he could get ready for his show, as if everything was cool. I grew irritated with his nonchalant behavior. He brushed it off stating that he had to work late so I could just come to the club and hang out with him there but I didn't want to. I was pregnant, and while I was just beginning to show I didn't feel the club was a place for a pregnant woman, even though it was for a comedy show. Besides, we had just officially gotten engaged, and I wanted to have an intimate celebration. I wanted time with Rodney all to myself, especially on Valentine's Day! We went back and forth about him not answering his phone. He claimed he was at work, but I wasn't buying it. My suspicions about him cheating began to resurface. I don't know if it was my hormones or intuition, but there wasn't anything in me that believed a word he spoke.

I told Rodney I wasn't going to the show, and he got upset but didn't make a huge deal like he normally would. Honestly, I was playing games with him. I planned on going, but I just wanted him to care that I wasn't going. He did care, but not enough. It's ironic that his mantrums annoyed me, but this night I wanted him to have one. I wanted him to be bothered that I didn't want to go out with him on Valentine's Day, hours after we got engaged.

He left, I showered and got ready. On my way out the door, I texted Rodney to let him know I was on my way. He simply replied, "Ok." Uneasy about his still nonchalant behavior, I headed to *The Master Plan*. Once I got there, he met me at the door as if nothing happened, kissed me on my lips, complimented me, and led me to my table. He knew I was coming and it was reassuring to see Rodney paid enough attention to actually know me, it definitely put me at ease. Maybe I was allowing my jealousy and insecurity to get the best of me after all, he wanted me there with him and it showed. After escorting me to my table at the front of the stage, he got me a water and told me he would return after the show began.

As I was sitting at the table sipping my water, vibing to the music watching passersby, a gentleman stopped briefly at my table and said, "Smile, don't look so mean." I tended to always look mean, but never on purpose. It was just my look so I laughed the half-hearted comment off. I guess it was his way of striking up a conversation with me because he proceeded to ask why I was there all alone. I told him I wasn't, flashed my ring and said my fiancé' was somewhere around here as I motioned around the club. I didn't know Rodney watched me from a distance as this short conversation was happening. The man respectfully bid me goodnight and continued on his way.

A few seconds after his departure, Rodney stormed up and shouted profanities at me asking who the guy was. Puzzled, I responded, "I don't know, just some random guy." That answer didn't suffice, and he became belligerent. I have always hated conflict of any kind and avoided it all costs. To avoid further embarrassment from Rodney's drunken public outburst, the runner in me got up from the table and headed to the bathroom in the back of the club with Rodney on my heels the entire time. Just as I was opening the bathroom door, which was across the hall from the storage room, he slammed it shut and I couldn't get in! He grabbed me and thrust me against the adjacent wall with his hands gripped around my throat. As this commotion was happening, I saw a guy friend, who I had grew up with for years, walk past and I pleaded for him to help me. Nonetheless, Rodney gave him the look of death and said, "Naw, she good." My "friend" just helplessly shrugged and walked away. That could have been a pivotal moment in the entire situation where someone, a man, stepped in to help but it wasn't as it only got worse and instead, he like the rest of the onlookers, walked by as if I were invisible.

People continued to walk by, as I continued to plead for help. I saw looks of sympathy, shock, indifference, but they just kept walking. None of them said one word to Rodney. Here I was in a hallway, being choked as Rodney accused me of screwing the guy who had stopped by the table, and yet no one cared enough to even call the police. I managed to reach in my jacket pocket and pull my phone out in order to dial 911. In breathy gasps, I said, "Help! My fiancé is trying to kill me!" Once he noticed I indeed call 911, he knocked the phone out of my hand and it fell to the floor. I fought to escape his ironclad grip, as he drug me into the storage room. The more I fought the tighter his hands gripped my neck seeming to crush my windpipe. I fell to the concrete floor of the dark, dank, and cold storage room. The lack of oxygen was wearing me down. I couldn't tell if I wasn't able to see because it was so dark or if I was losing consciousness. I still was trying to fight my way out the storage room. Each time I managed to tear myself from the floor, Rodney would kick me back to the ground with his heavy, tan boots. He slammed my head onto the concrete floor and that's when I gave up. I no longer attempted to get off the floor. Instead, I lay there in a fetal position trying to protect my belly as he continued to kick and stomp me. The storage room was empty so there was nothing for me to grab to defend myself. Eventually, I blacked out.

I was propelled back to consciousness by a pain that pierced my soul. My mind took me back to the cold, black and white, tile bathroom floor of a duplex we lived in as a child. I was three or four years old when my uncle kneeled over me, pulled my panties down and began rubbing petroleum jelly on my vagina. I gasped for air at the vivid memory and then lost consciousness again. Where were the paramedics?! I lay there tormented in my body and mind as I was flooded with old memories, but still fresh pain of my molestations. If I didn't think of a good thought, I would surely go hysterical! I combed through the recesses of mind, and I couldn't seem to find one good thought. Not one! Lord, please!!! Where are the medics?! I blacked out again waiting for the ambulance to come save us...me and my three-month fetus.

Suddenly, I was in the ambulance, temporarily blinded by bright lights and confused by medics asking me how much I had to drink. I hadn't drank at all. I heard the relieving sound of my baby's heart beating over the monitor and conversations about "The Fight" over the walkies of the emergency personnel onsite. It seemed that not only had my fiancé strangled and beat me in the storage room of the bar, he had also told everyone that I was a pregnant drunk before he left, *The Master Plan.* He was gone and nowhere to be found. I was alone in the back of an ambulance, pregnant, bruised, battered, broken, and half-crazy. Just when I thought my life was coming together, I felt the damaged goods of my life rotting to the core. I had so many highs and lows in one day and it was too much.

I traveled to the hospital in disbelief. Calmed by the sound of my baby's heartbeat; yet I was still in a state of shock. He had never physically abused me before this. The actual ride to the hospital was a blur, but the mental ride still plays vividly in my mind. My thoughts raced. Had I really become another statistic? Am I now a victim of domestic violence? Has my child's father left me before I even had the baby?! Why had this happened to me?! Wasn't I already damaged enough? At least my baby is ok? Or is that a good thing? My mind raced, but my thoughts weren't clear. So many thoughts and questions simply muddled any clarity, and I was thinking that having a baby by a complete maniac would bind me to him for life. In an attempt to quiet my racing and irrational thoughts, I did what I had learned to do so many times in tough situations, I prayed silently until we had arrived at the back entrance of the local hospital. Upon arrival, I was ushered into a private exam room where I was interrogated by hospital staff. It seemed the interrogation usurped my examination. Detectives quickly arrived and pictures were taken of my neck where minor bruises had begun to take form from the strength of Rodney's grip on my throat. Out of my line of vision, there was conversation between the exam nurse, detective, and other reporting personnel. Not being able to see them seemed odd and made me uncomfortable. They came over and asked me what had taken place at "The Master Plan." Full of emotion, I regurgitated the story, and they seemed to be in disbelief. The female detective asked, "What do you think made him so angry?" This infuriated me. I don't know if it was because I had already given them the story, or if it was because I felt she was implying I wasn't being truthful. Then, the male detective asked, "Have you had anything to drink?" I'm sure I let curse words fly! I felt insulted! I felt judged. It appeared as if they had already heard someone else's side and were being biased against me. At that point, I felt less like a victim and more like an offender, and I no longer wanted their help. I simply wanted to leave as quickly as possible and forget the entire night happened.

Chapter 9

Pop, Goes the Weasel!

The next few weeks were pretty quiet. Graduation was three months away, and I was preparing for my future along with making sure I carried my baby to term. I attempted to forget the Valentine's Day Massacre at The Master Plan, but my attempts were futile. I couldn't comprehend how Rodney could up and leave the baby and me. It wasn't that I needed him but I felt a sense of abandonment, loneliness, and with a void of reason as to why he would assault me. I wanted to know what triggered him to suddenly become abusive after being together for two years. I hadn't spoken to him in order to get any answers, but in true weasel fashion, he popped up.

After not hearing from Rodney for over a month, I received a call from a number I didn't recognize, and it was him. He spoke to me in his lower, sweeter, innocent, and less baritone voice as he tried to show some sense of regret. I didn't want to hear it. I only wanted to hear why he had snapped and where he had been all this time. The lame response he conjured up was, he blacked out and didn't really remember much from that night! Rodney only remembered asking me about the guy he had seen me talking to and then nothing else. I knew he was lying. I couldn't understand how he could only remember pieces and parts of that night everything leading up to him beating me in the back storage room as I was trying to protect my belly and not remember what happened next. Since his memory had failed him, I disclosed every gruesome detail. I wanted him to somehow feel at least a touch of the pain I felt. He began to cry and apologize stating he had too much to drink and would never intentionally hurt me or our child. In my naivety, I didn't know this was the routine for abusers to be so sympathetic and apologetic for the damage they caused so I believed him. I allowed his lies to stand up in front of me like a mirror, and I found myself remembering times when I too had blacked out after having too much to drink. My encounters with drunkenness hadn't turned violent, but I almost had an altercation with my close friend Renee. I was being drunk, belligerent and hot headed and if it wasn't for her level headed temperament we probably would have come to blows. Other than that one incident, I normally would just pass out. Reflecting changed my perspective because I was no saint either.

After talking for about an hour, Rodney informed me of his new job in Atlanta, and he wanted me, my daughter and our new baby to relocate after I graduated. While I wasn't fond of moving to Atlanta, I welcomed the idea. I wasn't sure if I still wanted to marry Rodney but decided I would figure that part out along the way. I can't say it was love at that point but more of an emotional attachment coupled with abandonment issues rooted in daddy issues. After my parents divorced, my father's visits became less and less frequent the older I got. Consequently, as I grew up, the more it seemed I needed and yearned for my father. Although there was a man in my life because of my mother's relationships, there is no bond on earth able to replace that of a biological father and daughter. I now admit, in hindsight, I had daddy issues. Only spending summers and some holidays with him caused me to have a problem with the separation process, especially if it wasn't on my terms. As a child, I always felt I had no say in my relationship with my father. I suppose that was "grown folks business" and no one considered me. So, if Rodney was not going to be in my life, I needed to be the person to determine when. I wouldn't accept him walking out on me the way that he did after *The Master Plan* incident.

If going to Atlanta led to ditching Rodney while seizing the opportunity to escape Toledo, I was fine with that because I would be in control of it and the separation would be on my terms. Spring Break was coming up, and he asked me to fly down for a visit first. Once I received the flight information, I saw that Rodney purchased a one-way ticket! He told me that he could only afford one way and would book my return flight after my arrival in Atlanta. I took the trip with immense hesitation and enough money in my pocket to get back home in case Rodney reneged on the ticket.

I was still warming up to the idea of seeing him again. The last time I had seen Rodney was when he sprinted out the door of the storage room at *The Master Plan* while I lay on the floor after he tried to kill me. I had second and third thoughts about what I was doing. He was in Atlanta; I was in Toledo, and free from the man who attempted to take the life of my unborn child and I. Years of damage bubbled up within me, and I had talked myself into willingly going back to him. I told myself that he had made a mistake, and I could be found guilty of mistakes too. I convinced myself I was overreacting and neither of us were perfect. I compelled myself to still have hope because he was damaged goods too. Being damaged goods was Rodney's saving grace with me.

I waited for two hours at the Atlanta airport with no communication from Rodney. Surely he didn't fly me down here to leave me at the airport! I was at my wits end when he arrived with a panicked look on his face. He claimed he had to deal with work issues, and then was stuck in traffic due to the downpour that was happening outside. I tried to accept his excuse and got into the car. On the drive, he informed me that we would be staying at a hotel because he didn't want his fiancé around his three roommates. I didn't want to be around a bunch of men anyway, but I found it odd that he waited until I got there to tell me. I got settled into the hotel and got ready for dinner. Afterwards, I was exhausted and we went to sleep. The next morning,

Rodney said he had to work, and this took me to the pinnacle of pissivity. Had I come all this way to be left in a hotel alone? Rodney hurried to get dressed and promised to return to the hotel for lunch. Lunch time came and went, and so did dinner time. I began calling Rodney, and like at the airport, my calls went unanswered. At that point, I was done. I didn't know what Rodney was doing, but I wasn't going to standby in a hotel room while he did it. I wanted to leave on the quickest flight. However, it was Spring Break and $200 would not be enough for an immediate one-way flight back home. I packed my bags, called the bus station and a cab instead.

Just as the cab arrived at 9 o'clock pm, Rodney walked through the door like leaving me alone all day was the original plan. Instantly, I demanded to know where he had been. When he noticed I had my jacket and shoes on with luggage in hand, his facial expression transformed from carefree to angry. We go back and forth for a while. He wanted to know what was wrong with me, and I wanted to know where he'd been. I realized we were going nowhere fast and was ready to storm out to the cab, but I hesitated remembering what happened the last time I stormed away from him. I made my best attempt to calm down and asked once more about his whereabouts. Before he could respond, I blurted all the things that had gone wrong with this trip. Then, I lied and told him I had spoken to Cherice who told me everything.

His face dropped, and instantly, that one lie that I had just told had revealed a whole lot of truth in that very moment. He was there in Atlanta with her! Just the expression on his face was enough to break me and send me to a whole different level of hurt. Hot tears began to stream down my face. He escaped from Toledo to Atlanta with her the night he assaulted me. For over a month afterwards, he didn't lift a finger to call to see if I or the baby was ok. Yet, the moment he did, I was willing to accept him back into my life. Thoughts of self-doubt, unworthiness and the lowest of low feelings began to flood my mind. What did he tell her the night of the assault? Why did he honor her? Does he physically and emotionally hurt her like he hurts me? Why am I not worthy of loyalty and love? Before I could drive the knife deeper into my own heart, Rodney began to explain. "I'm going to tell you everything and you can still leave if you want." he pleaded. I didn't get into the cab; I left with Rodney instead but I was still heading back o Toledo.

The ride to the bus station revealed just how much of a coward and weasel Rodney really was. He attempted to justify his disappearing act with a tale of how he needed Cherice the night after he attacked me so he could go to Atlanta. Rodney claimed she would make money by turning tricks for him until he could get a job that would not require a background check. He feared I would press charges, it would show up on a background check, and he had no intentions on turning himself in.

This is the same man who had told me weeks prior that he didn't remember anything about that night yet he somehow feared I would press charges. Interesting. Moreover, he went on to say how he was afraid I would send him to jail, but Cherice had his back. My mind was frazzled and I couldn't deal with his reasoning. He had strangled me, kicked me, punched me, slammed me on the floor, and left me there! I had no tolerance for the poison he was spewing. We parted ways and I headed home to Toledo with no plans on making things work with Rodney.

After a couple of months, my notions of not making it work with Rodney proved ineffectual. He called constantly with claims of having left Cherice for good since I had returned to Toledo. He wanted his family back and had hopes of creeping his way back into my life. He notified me of his plans to come back to Toledo and gave me daily updates on his job search. I entertained the conversations because I missed the good parts of our relationship, but I didn't miss all the chaos and hurt he brought into my life.

Even when I found out he had five children instead of two, I kept pressing forward. He fed me yet another excuse citing he wasn't sure if the youngest three were his due to the mother's lifestyle. Again, I still couldn't break away When we had discussed them moving to Ohio in the past, I didn't want them to. But now I welcomed the idea of his children moving to Ohio in hopes this would keep him settled, grounded and truly focused. Maybe it could work this time.

He moved back just in time for my college graduation but didn't attend the ceremony. A few days after graduation, I began my new job in the Labor and Delivery Department at one of the hospitals where I completed my clinical rotation. Unfortunately, just after completing orientation, I went into preterm labor. My water had broken during the beginning of my seventh month. I signed myself out after a few weeks in the hospital and opted for bed rest at home. Rodney was there to take care of me since no one else was around. It seemed like that was the normal for my family to be absent from my life when Rodney was present. I was able to hold out four more weeks before giving birth to our beautiful, baby girl.

Despite the countless, subsequent doctor visits that would reassure me everything was ok, the events from Valentine's Day still haunted my thoughts. After each visit, I still needed final confirmation my baby was healthy, and I finally received it the day she was born. Our daughter was born healthy and strong with no major issue or deficiencies, and for that I was grateful. I was emotional all night and the following day. I was so grateful that God had protected her in my womb in spite of the attack and stress. I wept. I knew why I was weeping but didn't want to share. I didn't feel strong enough to be vulnerable. So when my mother, the nurse or Rodney asked why I was sobbing, I simply responded, "I don't know" and tried to hold back the tears until I could thank God in private.

Murder Could've Been the Case

"…You know I'm not letting you leave me, right?"

Chapter 10

Murder Could've Been the Case

Things with Rodney and I were going well until they weren't. Honestly, I wasn't head over heels for him anymore. I just didn't know how or when to run away. To make matters worse, six months after having my baby girl, Rodney took me to have an outpatient surgical procedure. During the pre-op check in, the doctor entered my room to tell me I couldn't have the procedure because I was pregnant! This was after several fights, bloody noses, and attempts to run! I was horrified and I was not having another baby with Rodney. I just wasn't.

Rodney was in the room with me and seemed excited about the pregnancy. It was bad enough I was primarily supporting our child plus helping him to support the surprise five! Another baby wasn't going to happen. I was mortified and instantly asked my doctor if I should sue him or the drug company! He had put me on some new, chewable, birth control pill that clearly wasn't working because I was faithful in taking it. I wanted payback for the mental distress I anticipated Rodney was about to take me through since I refused to have this baby. I wasn't pro-abortion, but that was the only solution I could see.

If I had an abortion, Rodney threatened to mess me up and annihilate me. He was completely unhinged when I told him I wanted the abortion, that was a risk I was willing to take because I knew I was still going to do it. I came up with a plan to move to a neighboring county while Rodney was away in Atlanta. I still went to the office visits while simultaneously finding me a new apartment in the county I worked in. Additionally, I changed my number, found a moving crew and orchestrated the move so it happened the same weekend Rodney was out of town. My baby brother and his friends moved my things, and I got an abortion the next day. The physical, mental and emotional anguish I was sure to suffer under the hands of Rodney while pregnant, would break me. If I had to do this over again, I certainly would. I understood like never before the weight of this kind of decision. This was my situation and abortion was my choice. I have repented, and forgiven myself. My plan was executed effortlessly and I was finally free.

I was only living in the neighboring county so I still had to drive to Toledo to take my girls to Aunt Kim's house in the mornings. She took my oldest to school and watched the youngest while I worked. She lived in the same place for years and knew the neighborhood well. I began to notice a distinctively different car in her neighborhood. This was a newer model, pearl-colored Cadillac with a grey top sitting with the park lights on for the past two days. On the first day, I didn't say anything about it but I noticed. The second day, I asked my aunt who the car was waiting for and she looked out and said she didn't know. I brushed it off and went on about my evening. My new apartment was a locked building, so I felt more secure since I had to buzz people in. As soon as I unlocked the door holding our baby carrier in my arms, Rodney came out of nowhere and burst the door open before me. He had his friend, who he had "appointed" as our daughter's godfather, right behind him. Startled, I look straight past Rodney at his friend in disbelief. It always amazed me how his friends and family members stood by in the background as he terrorized me acting as if they had no clue what was going on. It was almost like they were afraid of him. No one was willing to tell him that he was out of line. I didn't want to go in, but I couldn't leave if I tried. Rodney had me cornered between going inside and going into his clasp. He was persistent in assuring me he just wanted to talk. He was speaking in his whiny, whisper voice with liquor on his breath. I was quite familiar with this tone, and I simply responded, "There is nothing to talk about Rodney, please leave." He wasn't backing down and I had no way out. All the while, his worthless friend was just standing there looking like a doofus. I went into the apartment and laid my baby in her crib. Gratefully, my older daughter was staying with Aunt Kim this night because I was off the next day. Rodney's friend made himself comfortable on the couch, as Rodney instructed, and I proceeded to the bedroom to get ready for the shower.

I was bleeding and still spotting from the abortion. It seemed the stress of the situation had caused me to pass a few, unexpected blood clots and I only had on a panty liner. All I wanted to do was get out of my clothes and into a shower. He interrogated me with questions, "Are you hiding from me?! You trying to get away from me? You know I'm not letting you leave me, right?" I gave him half-hearted responses as I prepared my water, towel, night clothes, and most importantly, my mind for the fight and conversation I foresaw was about to happen. Even if I tried to hide it, I knew he would ask if I had an abortion since there was blood in my panties. I was paranoid, but tried to be strategic in making moves because he was watching me like a hawk. I grabbed all my things and headed to the bathroom with Rodney on my heels. I tried to close the door and asked for a little privacy, but he wouldn't relent. I opted for a bath instead of a shower. I ran a hot bath, got into the water, and was in disbelief at what he was doing. Rodney was undressing to get in the tub with me! I asked, "Rodney! What are you doing? I am about to take a bath it has been a long day and I'm not feeling well."

Rodney said with an eerie calmness, "I'm about to get in there with you." As hot as the water was, my whole entire body shivered with chills as Rodney got in the tub and stood behind me. I instantly prayed for the Lord to protect me. Beneath Rodney's faux calmness, I felt his energy. I knew something was brewing. We had NEVER taken a bath together...NEVER. The next words Rodney uttered chilled me even more. I wanted to lie. I wanted to run. I wanted to scream. If I did, who would hear me other than my helpless baby? Rodney's worthless friend would probably help him hide the body if it came to that. Rodney gripped my bare shoulders, "Did you kill my baby?" He moved his hands closer towards my neck thrusting me in a downward motion as he began to lean his body weight in on me, in an attempt to submerge me under the water. I hopped out of that tub screaming and crying. I think I saw my life flash before my eyes.

Rodney chased me into the bedroom and proceeded to rape me even though I was still recovering from the abortion. I didn't fight, because I had learned fighting back only made it worse. I took it, and laid there next to him silent, numb and tired. Tired of fighting. Tired of wanting to run. Tired of failing. Tired of being afraid. Tired of being my own worst enemy. It was another February and I was being damaged yet again. I prayed hard that night and asked God to please take him away from me forever, even if it meant death. I feared for my life and couldn't figure out a way to safely remove myself from the situation. After I finished praying, Rodney was fast asleep, as well as our daughter and his friend who was sleeping on the couch.

I just wanted to leave them there, but where would I go? There was no escaping him. The thought of a shelter was a joke. I still had to make a living for me and my children. I went to the kitchen and got a knife and figured if he wouldn't let me leave, I would just kill him. My Auntie Kim will take care of my kids. At this point, it's self-defense or temporary insanity. I stood over him, staring while recalling all he had put me through. I began to sob. I wasn't a murderer. I did not have the heart to kill him. I was a lover whose heart's desire was to be loved back. I slid the knife under my mattress and went to sleep.

I arose at 7 A.M. the next morning while everyone was still asleep, and drove straight to the police station to file a police report in this new county. I didn't have any witnesses, but they had access to my previous county's records. I told them everything and was able to stand before the judge to get the temporary protection order that morning. I walked back into my house and told him, "You have 5 minutes to get out of my house, the police are on their way. I just left the police station and I have a protection order in both counties for me, and both of my children. Your paperwork is in the mail." I was done. It was over, I was FREE....

Chapter 11

Unworthy

The next few months would be cold, quiet and a bit lonely. For a time, I was ok with that. While I lived in a bit of fear, wondering when Rodney would come back, I also found peace in being alone. While the months seemed cold and long, our time apart did not last long. I began to answer his calls, mostly because I never wanted to be the mother who denied a man the right to be in their child's life. Our child was the glue that kept us together. I had some peace of mind knowing if he lifted a finger against me, the police would be there to lock him up within minutes because of the restraining order, or at least I hoped so. We weren't the same though. I wasn't all in but I went through the motions and settled for the hand of love I was dealt since it was what I thought I deserved. Rodney remained jealous with a cheating heart and I had reached the point where I didn't care much. I had become institutionalized in some way. Being locked into him, although horrendous, it was familiar. While being free of him was foreign.

Rodney's other five children came to stay with us during the summer until their mother got settled into Ohio. According to Rodney, they had moved up from Atlanta so he could be closer to all of his children. The presence of his children seemed to ease the burden of our relationship, but it was far from the life I wanted for myself. Never in a million years had I dreamed of becoming a mother of two, step-mother of five, and a wife to an unfaithful, abusive man. The Lord must have had something better in store for me, or did He **not**? Was I so damaged that no one worth having would want me? Was I even worthy of having a man devoid of the drama? Probably not...at least that was my thought process at the time.

After years of being picked on, talked about, and even made to feel less than by my brothers, friends and classmates, I had built up my confidence by reading self-help books over the years. The books often contained scriptures from Psalms and Proverb that spoke to my soul. Somehow along the way, I managed to allow myself to get back down in the murky mud made of unworthiness, but this time, I was fine wallowing there for a while. Honestly, I was tired of fighting.

Rodney wasn't the ideal companion, but I was beginning to become settled with the idea of making it work. I had actually come to the conclusion that maybe all God had in store for me was to attend AA meetings with Rodney, be a mother of seven and be his savior wife at the tender age of 26.

The abuse had ended once Rodney became clean from drinking and that made life easier. He still had his moments where he would be insecure. He would pop up at my job when I didn't answer my phone or accuse me of being with another man. Even though his insecurity and accusations didn't result in physical assault, it did lead me back to smoking cigarettes and cigars. When my co-workers went out for a smoke break, I soon followed. I went from a closet, social smoker to an "I don't care who sees me or judges me. I need nicotine to calm my nerves smoker." However, I never did it around my children. I cared enough about their image of me but no one else mattered. As damaged as I was and unworthy as I felt, I didn't want to taint or damage my girls' image of me. I knew the truth though.

I was tainted. Soiled by my uncle at the age of 3 or 4, gradually having my innocence ripped away between the ages of 9 to 11, and by the time I had become a sexually-active adult, I couldn't begin to identify what a healthy, sexual relationship was. Compound all that with the daddy issues that I harbored after my father left when I was 5 and only showing up on holidays, I was broken. The rejection I felt from my father's refusal to take me in after my mother kicked me out, was probably the sledgehammer that shattered my self-worth. If my own biological father didn't want me, even with no financial obligations, why was I worthy of any other man now?! The damages were very deep for me. I only felt I was worthy of what I currently had.

I spent my life trying to be a better role model than my mother was but consistently fell short and somehow I ended up being a reincarnated version of her. I was in an abusive relationship, imprisoned mentally and physically by a man who I felt was the only man I deserved. Despite my prayers and hopes for deliverance from this depressive life, I stayed.

Easter Sunday was a day I'll never forget. I had to work and Rodney had been out visiting his family with our daughter and his other kids all day. I stopped by his mother's house to pick him up so we could head to his uncle's house for dinner. However, we got into an argument. I could tell from the stench flowing from his pores, he had been drinking again. When I brought up his drinking and accused him of going back to his old ways, he became belligerent and attempted to take the steering wheel from me while I was driving. Because of this, he almost wrecked the car! In a panic, I pulled over at the gas station and Rodney got out screaming obscenities at me. I was shaking. He could have killed all of us including our 8-month old baby, who was resting in the back seat. I left him at the gas station, and drove home frantically in awe of what had just happened. I had become nervous wondering if Rodney would show up to my door drunk and belligerent later that night.

Rodney never showed up, but I received a phone call in the wee hours of the morning from his friend telling me Rodney had been taken to jail. In total shock, I hastily began to call family and friends who might know what happened but everyone acted as if they knew nothing. Something inside told me to turn on the news as I waited for his call. I watched the news update reels from the night before and patiently waited for the newscasters to possibly provide more information on what Rodney was booked for. I wasn't really expecting him to make the news, but something in my gut told me that maybe there was a chance that whatever had happened would show up on the news. All sorts of stories came into my mind about how his hot-head and quick-temper combined with alcohol had gotten him in a situation that he wasn't able to talk his way out of. Maybe he was in jail for drunk driving or even indecent exposure again. I was grasping at straws and I was ready to give up on guessing. Right then I heard, "A Toledo man is in custody on charges of kidnapping and felonious assault, and it all happened here at this apartment."

As the newscaster began to recite the name and the details of the encounter, I began to feel sick! Even before they uttered the name Rodney Russell, I knew in my heart he was the assailant in a gruesome crime of passion. The newscaster stated Rodney had refused to leave the woman's apartment and held her against her will. He used his belt to strangle her while inflicting several wounds to restrain her and hold her hostage. The woman waited for Rodney to pass out before she escaped and called the police. The circumstances surrounding the entire ordeal were familiar to me and seemed like déjà vu.

It reminded me of the time when Rodney had forced his way into my apartment awhile and became violent. I waited for him to go to sleep and woke up early in the morning and went to the courthouse to press charges and get a restraining order. However, shortly after that occurrence when Rodney had pulled another one of his disappearing acts for a while and he'd left to be with Cherice, she called me looking for him! While he wasn't with me, she and I conversed about his possessiveness and how he wouldn't leave either of us alone. During our conversation, I told Cherice about the time when I had given up on fighting him, waited until he fell asleep, woke up the next morning and went to the police station to file a restraining order on him in hopes to put some distance between the two of us.

Cherice was the woman on the news! She had done exactly what I did when I got the restraining order a few months back when Rodney forced his way into my apartment, but she used it to land Rodney in jail! I didn't know how to feel. I was flooded with anger, disgust, and then guilt. Had I failed Rodney and then given Cherice exactly what she needed to lock him away for good? Or had I done exactly what I needed to do to free us both? My mind was in disarray. Even after the initial shock of it all, I still couldn't begin to process everything.

Rodney was held at the local county jail for a few weeks before he was released on bail to await trial. During that time, I helped to get him a lawyer and made sure to not talk to anyone about what I did or did not know about the case. Rodney was facing 25 years regarding this case and while it was all as a result to his actions and betrayal toward me, somehow, I felt the need to be there for him. After all, he was my child's father and had five other children to be there for.

Rodney laid low while he was out on bond. He was spending time with family and friends, mostly me and the kids, and trying to keep himself out of trouble. When the time for sentencing finally came, my prayer was "Lord let thy will be done" so Rodney took a plea deal. With the letter written by me, business associates and others, he pretty much received a slap on the wrist for the crime committed. I cried when he was sentenced but in my heart I already knew his fate, part of me was really crying for Cherice because I felt like I had sold my soul to the devil for fighting for him instead of fighting for her as a fellow victim of domestic violence. That moment in the courtroom haunted me and I felt like a coward, like the biggest imposter. But at the same time, I felt like I was doing what I was supposed to do for my child. Who tells us what we are supposed to do in situations like this?! I began to hate myself even more during this time and it showed. I felt I had reached the point of no return so while I was technically finally free from Rodney for 3 years, I had no more desire to go anywhere so I guess you can say that I had become an addict of my own pain.

He's Locked Up but, Am I Free

I went to see Rodney monthly while he was in jail and the more I made that long, hour and a half drive, the more time I had to slowly talk myself into making the visits further and further apart. Rodney began to pressure me into marrying him in jail and I simply wasn't having it. That was where I drew the line. Even worse, he had been claiming that his friends and cousins were writing and telling him that they had been seeing me around town with different guys, which were all lies. I was tired of the lies, manipulations and games so eventually the visits and the letters stopped. I needed a break from Rodney, if nothing else just to clear my head.

By winter, I was finally back to getting dressed up, going out and having a good time. If I was going to stay in Toledo, I sure as heck wasn't going to stay in hiding. Sheila and I were back to hanging out and I had actually met someone else. His name was Miles, and with no real intention of being anything more than friends we soon crossed the line. We went from partying together as a group to spending more and more time alone which began to completely complicate things. I wasn't emotionally ready to be wrapped up in anyone else nor did I have intentions on doing so but it happened.

After several months of my lackluster efforts to reciprocate Rodney's attempts to communicate, with his threats of "If you don't marry me, we don't need to be together." Then, him recanting his statements by following them up with "You're my wife forever...no matter what," I eventually broke down and went to see him. Rodney wanted desperately for me to marry him while he was in jail, and I was not going for it. I had no problem supporting him but I had no plans on marrying Rodney whether he was locked up or free.

To this day, I don't know why I chose to support him, even in this. I can only attribute it to my feelings of unworthiness and my seeking to redeem myself by proving I could be his pseudo savior. I wanted to prove I was the woman who was there for him, regardless of all that he had taken me through. I didn't want to be the one who gave up on him. Surely if I proved that I could be strong for him, he would turn his life around and live right. I felt myself becoming more distant from the reality of who I was and less self-aware. I fantasized about the fairytale life we would share after this was all over based on the potential of a man who had shown me nothing more than who he really was. I was so damaged that I stopped seeing me.

The Thursday before Labor Day, I made the drive to see Rodney. I was feeling mixed emotions because I had dated someone else for the first time in years and now I was on the road to see Rodney. When I arrived, he was excited and emotional because he had received some exciting news that he was eager to share with me. Nonetheless, I was emotionally distant. Rodney sensed my distance during the visit. He had perpetually accused me of cheating when I did nothing wrong, but I think he finally knew that after all of his false accusations, I had in fact been with someone else this time. And I was fine with that. At that point, I wasn't sure how much longer I could support Rodney or be his girlfriend. However, I did want to continue to support him as the mother of his child.

When he put the pieces together, he went ahead and shared his good news. The news he shared with me was the nail in the coffin that I had been lying in for years. I kept resurrecting, but this news sealed this part of my life for good. "Since you aren't going to marry me, me and Crystal are going to get married," as he handed me a folded piece of paper. I'm not sure what I expected it to be, but it was a paternity test. He continued, "I was so excited to tell you the new baby boy wasn't mine, and this is how you do me?" As I held our daughter, I sat there in disbelief, balling with soundless, crocodile tears streaming down my face. I had no idea he had been cheating with and was planning to marry the mother of his other children too. I didn't know what hurt more, the cheating, the engagement, or how he effortlessly told me. All I knew was that it hurt He was so eager and proud to show me the test as if it would make me happy but I wasn't happy at all! I was sitting there crying and dumbfounded because I never for one moment suspected he had been cheating with her. She would regularly insist that she respected my relationship with Rodney. They never seemed overly friendly and she often welcomed me into her home for cordial conversations. Crystal and I were not friends but maintained a healthy relationship for the sake of the children however, unbeknownst to me, she was sleeping with Rodney and smiling in my face. I was indeed naive but I never saw this one coming.

It may seem that the brutal attack against Cherice would've been the last straw to force me to walk away from Rodney, but it wasn't. Perhaps, the rape or the beating at The Master Plan would have been enough but none of that had driven me to leave. Maybe it should have been the fact that I was required to sleep with my keys in my panties and my daughter strapped into her car seat in case we had to run, but it wasn't. It was the fact that I allowed him to believe I was so worthless and gave him license to treat me as such. My thoughts raced. Rodney had cheated, stolen from me, beaten me and I still loved him. Did I just love myself less and less with every strike to my self-worth? I loved him harder and harder thinking I could love the damages out of him becoming more damaged the longer I stayed in the relationship. As I poured love into him, life was sucked out of me. I was attempting to pour from a very dry, barren and scorched place. I felt how bad off I was when he so easily said that he and Crystal were getting married despite the fact that her newborn child was not his.

I couldn't comprehend why he had come into my life to begin with? Why he came to shake up my world and suck the life right out of me when I was on target to obtaining the future I desired? The visit came to an end. I wiped my tears, held my daughter close, and didn't say goodbye. It didn't come in the way that I had expected it, but maybe after all of those sleepless nights and cries out to God, my prayers had finally been answered despite how bad it hurt. I left the prison shaken, broken but with my head held high. I knew that was the last time that I would ever see Rodney.

From Pieces to Peace: Forgiving the Unforgivable

Preview

I spent my life being good and doing well only to often feel the walls crashing down on me, to have people walk away from me and give up on me. Don't get me wrong, I do not claim to have been a saint by any stretch of the imagination. However, I spent tireless years of my life trying to release myself from the generational curses and infirmities that plagued my life but was unsuccessful. I often cried out to God for answers and because I did not hear a response went about things my way, often finding myself in bad situations time after time. After leaving Rodney, I was determined things would be different, no more doing things my way, or at least that was the plan.

Once I got into my car, I called my close friend, Tori. She had moved to Orangeburg, South Carolina after high school, in Michigan, to go to college. She was the sister I never had so we kept in touch throughout the years. When she answered the phone, fresh tears began to flow, and I let Tori know I was finally ready to leave. The pain of that day brought back so much pain that Rodney hadn't even caused. Tori asked, "So what are you gonna do?" She didn't give me a day or two to think about it nor allow me to feel sorry for myself. She didn't waste any time. I replied "I'm ready to leave now." That was all I had to say. She welcomed the idea of me moving to South Carolina and that was all I desired because I wanted to get out of Toledo. It was under unconventional circumstances, and I may have taken the long road, but I would be delivered from both Rodney's grasp and the streets of the city that were growing desolate by the day. A prayer that I thought had gone unanswered for years had just been answered, in a way that I never saw coming. Yes, I was damaged goods but I saw in that moment, despite all of the abuse, all of the hurt, all of the bad choices, all it takes is ONE. One moment, one person, one positive choice, one act of kindness, one person believing in me to salvage what I thought was lost. That day, that one person was Tori. She helped awaken that thing on the inside of me, over the course of my new journey, and there would be many more. What is important is somewhere, along the way, I had to become my own one. My own person. I left for South Carolina, determined to follow a new roadmap.

The trip to Charleston was exciting, yet terrifying! I had no idea what to expect. While I had excitement on the outside, Tori could sense my fear. She did her best to make it a fun and mindless trip. We didn't talk about Rodney or the horrors that I had been through, or the things I had to look forward to. Here I was free, and on the road to newness; yet, I was secretly hurting as I was heading to start my new life. I needed to be delivered, from him. I realized this would take some serious time, intervention, and undoing that I couldn't do on my own.

After three months of being in Charleston, I met this sweet, jovial woman at my job named Jewel. I could tell Jewel was different. I felt drawn to her instantly so I sat down with her at lunch and we immediately began chatting. During the course of lunch, we learned a lot about one another, and I could sense that I could trust her immediately. She had a very welcoming, honest, loving and trusting spirit. Jewel and I were complete opposites. She was a single socialite, from the southwest who attended a major university in Arizona. She was a fitness junkie and was spiritually grounded. I, on the other hand, was a single mother of two, with an Associates degree, a party animal, no spiritual grounding and had never seen the inside of a gym. I knew I needed a friend and Jewel knew I needed someone too. So we exchanged numbers with plans to hang out in the near future.

Over one of our dinner outings, she invited me to church. Jewel was always happy, smiling, uplifting and never, ever had anything negative to say which made me curious. When we were out she would receive compliments about how people could see the God in her and I yearned for that, as people often could sense the strife in my life. I must admit, at first, my heart was so hard, Jewel's personality annoyed even me. But as my heart soften and I let God in, I became much like a "Jewel", much like her in spirit, in a sense and people began to see the God in me.

Visiting Jewel's church was an experience like one I had never experienced before. As soon as I walked through the door, I felt love, not condemnation. Most importantly, I gained the tools to help overcome all of the bitterness, hurt, brokenness, and unforgiveness I harbored in my heart. That's when I committed my life to Christ on my own as an adult. I began to seek Him for myself and see Him through my own lens, instead of the religion and tradition that had been forced upon me during my childhood. Up until then, there was so much chaos, bitterness, blame-shifting and drama going on in my life, that I failed to totally trust God, gain my own understanding of who He is or develop a personal relationship with Him. I learned that I had to surrender the pieces of my life over to God in order to really begin the journey toward peace and wholeness. That was what I was missing. I knew I had been living wrong but I wasn't ready to start the forgiveness part of the journey until I received salvation. In fact, I didn't realize I had to forgive nor did I know how much to forgive. All that I had endured in life required me to forgive everything in order for me to heal. All the abuse, trauma, drama, bitterness, lovelessness, self-loathing, and grief. How would I manage to forgive the unforgivable?

Made in the USA
Middletown, DE
29 April 2018